Greenwich Council
Library & Information Service

IN HOUSE
QUALITY
SYSTEMS

Blackheath Library
Old Dover Road, SE3 7BT
020 8858 1131

Please return by the last date shown

3 0 JUL 2009

- 3 SEP 2009

1 6 OCT 2009

6 NOV 2009

2 6 APR 2010

Thank
You!

To renew, please contact any Greenwich library

Issue: 02   Issue Date: 06.06.00   P 6 PM RBL LIS

Text and Illustrations © John Franklin 1997
Design and layout Terry Marle © The Stationery Office 1997
An earlier edition of this book was published by Unwin Paperbacks in 1988
This edition first published in 1997 by The Stationery Office Limited

Applications for reproduction should be made in writing to The Stationery
Office Copyright Unit, St Crispins, Duke Street, Norwich NR3 1PD

John Franklin has asserted his right under the Copyright, Designs and
Patents Act 1988 to be identified as Author of this Work

ISBN 0 11 702051 6

British Library Cataloguing in Publication Data

A CIP catalogue record for this book is available from the British Library

Printed in the UK for The Stationery Office by Reflex Litho Ltd

J16457, 6/97, C100, 562079, 72958

About the author

John Franklin has been closely involved in cycle planning and safety activities for more than twenty years. Registered as an Expert Witness on cycling techniques and proficiency, he is called upon to advise on matters concerning the use of highways by cyclists.

Actively involved in cycling issues from national to local levels, John is Chairman of the Cycle Campaign Network, Buckinghamshire County Representative for Cyclists' Touring Club (CTC) and Secretary of Milton Keynes Cycle Users' Group. He is a past member of the CTC's National Council and was instrumental in establishing its modern cycle planning activities. John has also represented cyclists on road safety advisory committees in London and Milton Keynes.

A cyclist of wide experience who cycles as his primary means of transport and for leisure, the author has cycled extensively under all kinds of conditions throughout Britain, Europe and farther afield. He is married with two children, and all his family cycle regularly.

Contents

List of figures

List of tables

Introduction

Cycling for health, safety and you

Cycling is undergoing a great revival and many people would like to cycle or to cycle more. However, the traditional myths that cycling is hard work and slow have been augmented in recent years by the perception that cycling is also inevitably dangerous. Many people fear riding in today's traffic, on roads too often designed primarily for motor vehicles, and feel that there is little cyclists can do to protect themselves from the dangers present.

Experienced cyclists know otherwise. They know that by controlling their machine correctly and using appropriate riding techniques, cycling can not only be safe but also fun. Learning to ride efficiently means that cycling is seldom strenuous and is frequently a speedy means of getting about, particularly in towns. One of the biggest problems for someone learning to cycle is overcoming the prejudices and misconceptions which have for too long been a part of cycling folklore.

In fact, far from being an unsafe activity, research shows that cycling regularly is twenty times more likely to increase your life span than to shorten it. Cyclists, on average, live some seven years longer than non-cyclists, and in particular they are twelve times less likely to die of heart disease. Whatever the negative effects of sharing the roads with heavy traffic or of breathing in fumes, it is evident that, on balance, cycling leads to longer and healthier lives. Moreover, when you choose to cycle rather than to travel by car, everyone benefits from reductions in pollution and congestion.

If you learn to cycle skillfully you will enhance your ability to use the roads in safety. Although you may encounter much bad driving, most of it is foreseeable and avoidable. Accordingly, this book has banished the word 'accident', for few crashes fall into that category. A number of surveys suggest that competent cyclists are ten times less likely to be involved in a conflict, and crash rate generally decreases with a rider's experience.

How Cyclecraft *can help you to cycle well*

Skilled cycling technique is seldom taught, at least not beyond the basics covered by proficiency schemes for children. Cycling families pass skills down from generation to generation, whilst people who ride with cycling clubs benefit from seeing how others tackle particular situations. For adults without such connections, however, the little advice available is too often negative and unrealistic.

Cyclecraft teaches cycling technique in a similar way to teaching an adult to drive a car – how to integrate with traffic, not fear it. The general aims are to maximise your safety and riding efficiency, whilst minimising inconvenience to others and wear to your machine.

Advice is given on how to deal with all common road situations, recognising how impractical it often is to avoid the more difficult ones. It follows the supposition, well endorsed by skilled riders, that the only way to be safe is to learn to control a cycle as a vehicle and to read and respond to what is going on around you. For this reason the cyclist is frequently referred to as a vehicle driver, for that is what you must be. *Cyclecraft* also outlines the problems experienced by other road users; by taking these into account, you can react in ways most likely to enhance your journey.

This book makes no attempt to excuse the bad behaviour which is sometimes evident on today's roads, nor to excuse those road designs which can increase disproportionately the risks for more vulnerable road users. Priorities are changing and conditions for cycling should improve, but in the mean time it is necessary for anyone wishing to cycle to come to terms with present circumstances. There is also little doubt that most cyclists could do more to make themselves safer, for they often make conditions more difficult than they need be. Although motorists are most often primarily at fault in crashes with adult cyclists, very often conflicts could be avoided altogether by the cyclist riding more diligently. *Cyclecraft* therefore concentrates on how to deal with the existing order, rather than lamenting the fact that conditions could be better.

Cyclecraft is *not* concerned with setting examples to others. Although a skilled rider will often do this as a matter of course, a cyclist is too vulnerable to follow rigid rules irrespective of the danger. *Cyclecraft* shows how to respond to actual conditions, not to a rule book.

Cyclecraft's *readership*

Cyclecraft is aimed specifically at adults. Whilst many of the basic techniques are suitable for children, the more complicated manoeuvres, which involve the judgement of conditions and of the intentions of others, are not. Because of their underdeveloped road sense, children generally need to be taught a more submissive style of cycling which avoids the need to make quick or complex decisions.

The advice given in *Cyclecraft* applies to all types of cycle in common use today, although the limitations of some may militate against tackling some of the most difficult manoeuvres. Chapter 1 compares the characteristics of the various types of machines, and other chapters refer to significant differences in riding technique. Chapter 12 gives specific detail about riding tandems, tricycles and recumbents. For most of the book, however, the use of a large-wheel, multi-geared hybrid, sports or touring cycle is assumed, as these types are the most versatile in all on-road situations.

Using Cyclecraft

Cyclecraft follows a structured approach. Starting by ensuring that the bicycle is correctly adjusted to suit its rider, the book then gives a thorough grounding in basic cycling skills before dealing with on-road situations of increasing complexity. It is strongly recommended that you follow the book systematically: complete competence in the earlier skills is essential before more complicated manoeuvres can be carried out successfully.

Most adults of reasonable fitness should be capable of acquiring these skills, but you should take care not to proceed too quickly, nor beyond your capabilities at any time. Gradual acclimatisation to cycling in traffic is the best approach, getting used to more demanding traffic situations one by one. People who are particularly slow, timid or nervous may be unable to attain the more advanced skills without patience and perseverance.

Safety first

Before proceeding to the substance of *Cyclecraft*, an important caution: increased skill can lead to greater adventurousness, which may offset gains in safety. Be aware of this, and avoid complacency at all times.

1 —— A safe and efficient bike

For safe, efficient and enjoyable cycling, your bicycle should be suited to the uses you will make of it. There must be a good fit between it and its rider, and the cycle needs to be adjusted to perform properly. A good bike, well suited to its rider and regularly maintained, will give many years of satisfying service, allowing cycle and cyclist to operate as one, the machine almost being an extension of the limbs of its rider.

However, a bad match or poor adjustment will at best lead to disappointment and disillusionment with cycling; at worst it could result in a bad spill in traffic. Bear in mind that even a multiplicity of approval marks does not signify a safe bike if the size is wrong or if it has not been set up correctly.

This chapter discusses the various types of bicycle that are available, explains the parts of a cycle which are important for safety and efficiency, and gives brief notes on adjustments for optimum performance. However, it cannot tell you in detail how to adjust your particular bike, as individual components and their adjustment vary so much. For more information on your specific model, refer to a detailed repair manual or get help from an experienced cyclist or a cycle dealer.

Which type of bike?

Just as there are many types of cyclists and many reasons why people cycle, so there are many types of cycle, each best suited to particular circumstances.

The traditional **roadster** bicycle with curved handlebars is still in use, though it is now much less common in Britain than in many other countries. It is robust and reliable, but also heavy, which restricts its ability to keep pace with traffic even over short distances.

Small-wheel bicycles are popular with many people. They can be very manoeuvrable and stable, and have the special advantage of being readily adaptable in size to a number of users. Some can be folded, which is particularly useful for commuting by public transport. Some up-market models have many of the attributes of a sports cycle, but most others are inefficient and suited only to cycling short distances.

The **mountain** or **all-terrain bike** (ATB) has broad wheels and almost straight handlebars. Originally developed for use off-road, where it has particular advantages in terms of grip, robustness and comfort on rough tracks, this type of bike has also become popular for general use in both town and country. On-road their main attribute is greater resilience where surfaces are worn or pot-holed; on the other hand, these cycles are sluggish and poorly suited to manoeuvring in traffic. ATBs are not the best choice for most people's cycling needs, but may be improved for road use by fitting narrower tyres and bar ends.

A variant of the ATB, the **hybrid** or **city bike**, is better suited to town cycling and touring, with enhanced performance, full mudguards, a carrier and road-style tyres. There is a choice of handlebar designs – choose one with alternative holding positions and without protrusions that could catch on anything.

The **sports** or **touring style** of bicycle is often, mistakenly, referred to as a racing bike. However, there are wide differences in specification, and most models are not intended for competitive activities. This type of cycle – usually but not necessarily with dropped handlebars – has declined in popularity in recent years, but is well suited to both commuter cycling and touring. Good manoeuvrability and efficiency make it ideal for integrating with traffic, although derailleur-type gears are not the best suited to stop-start traffic. High-pressure tyres increase efficiency, a benefit over longer distances, but are much less tolerant of poor surfaces and typical off-road conditions.

Still rare but growing in popularity are **recumbent** cycles, which come in a wide variety of designs. These offer the best combination of efficiency and comfort, and are very stable, with a low centre of gravity. The 'laid-back' position of the rider is of special benefit to people with back problems, whilst there are also safety advantages in riding feet, rather than head, first.

Tricycles are becoming more popular as utility machines, and provide a solution for people who cannot balance well on a bicycle. They are useful for carrying shopping and children. Riding a tricycle requires different skills from riding a bicycle, especially when turning. Their stability is an advantage in traffic, but they are less manoeuvrable where roads are congested.

Tandems and **tandem tricycles** are a great way for two people to travel together, particularly if one rider is stronger than the other. Children and visually-impaired people may ride as tandem partners with adults or those with normal sight. These machines are generally akin to sports bicycles, although ATB and recumbent tandems are also available.

The special skills required for riding tandems, trikes and recumbents are dealt with in Chapter 12.

The parts of a cycle

Figure 1.1 illustrates the location of the parts of a cycle, using a sports cycle as an example. Figure 1.2 shows the angles of a cycle to which reference is made.

Frame

The most fundamental specification of a bicycle is its **frame** size, which determines all the basic dimensions of the machine. If this is wrong, there is really nothing that can be done except to buy a new bike. The frame size should be large enough so that the handlebar stem and seatpin do not protrude more than is safe from the frame, whilst it should be small enough to permit you to straddle the topmost tube safely with both feet flat on the ground when stopped. The distance between the saddle and handlebars, which varies with frame size, should enable a comfortable riding position which neither cramps the body nor makes it difficult to operate the brakes.

A good starting point is to select a frame size 23–25 cm (9–10 inches) smaller than your inside leg measurement from crotch to floor, without shoes. Then, because there will still be slight variations in length and other parameters, try several frames of this size – with saddle and handlebars adjusted as described below – until you find the best fit. Good cycle dealers are usually

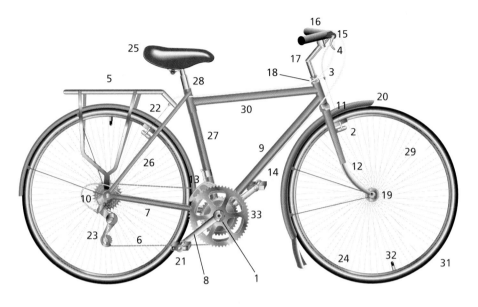

Figure 1.1
The parts of a hybrid bicycle

1	bottom bracket	18	headset
2	brake block in shoe	19	hub
3	brake cables	20	mudguard
4	brake levers	21	pedal
5	carrier	22	rear brake
6	chain	23	rear gear (derailleur)
7	chain stays	24	wheel rim
8	crank	25	saddle
9	down tube	26	seat stays
10	freewheel	27	seat tube
11	front brake	28	seatpin
12	front forks	29	spokes
13	front gear	30	top tube
14	gear cables	31	tyre
15	gear levers	32	valve (part of inner tube)
16	handlebars	33	chainwheel(s)
17	handlebar stem		

Figure 1.2
The frame and its geometry

a   seat tube angle
b   front fork rake
c   head tube angle

happy for you to road-test a number of models in this way.

There are three important aspects of the geometry of a frame that require a compromise between comfort and efficiency. These are the **seat tube angle** (a in fig 1.2), the **head tube angle** (c in fig 1.2) and the **front fork rake** (b in fig 1.2). The two angles represent the inclination of their respective tubes to the horizontal, whilst the front fork rate is a measure of the amount the front forks sweep forward from top to bottom. Between them, these three parameters determine the overall length, or wheelbase, of a cycle. The larger the wheelbase, the better a cycle evens out the bumps of the road, but the less efficient it is at accelerating.

Seat and head tube angles of 72° or 73° are best for both town riding and touring: steeper angles are ideal for racing but not really suitable for other uses. As to the front fork rake, for a non-competitive bike the most important consideration is to ensure that the rake is sufficient that the pedals, even if fitted with toe clips, cannot hit the front mudguard on sharp corners.

Saddle and handlebars

There are three adjustments to be made to the saddle: height, horizontal position and tilt (Figure 1.3). The ease and precision with which these adjustments may be made varies according to the type of seatpin, and all three interact.

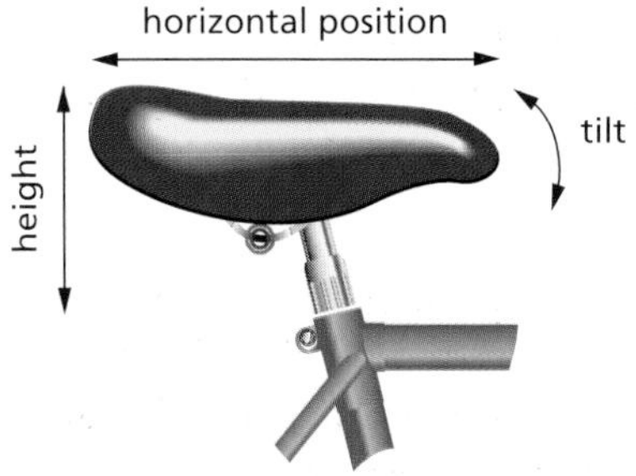

Figure 1.3
Saddle adjustments

The **saddle height** is set to permit the maximum transfer of energy from foot to pedal by allowing your foot to descend as great a distance as possible on each stroke with your leg as near straight as possible, whilst at the same time allowing your foot to remain in good contact with the pedal for its full 360° rotation. In theory this means that the saddle should be as high as possible without your feet losing contact with the pedals, but in practice a slightly lower position is necessary to enable you to put a foot on the ground comfortably when stopped.

The usual rule for adjustment is to set the saddle height so that the heel of your foot can just rest on the pedal with your leg fully stretched (Figure 1.4). This is not how you will ride, but allows for the flexing of your knee as you do. If you are new to cycling, a saddle set slightly lower than this may give you more confidence at first, but don't forget to raise it later. As well as being inefficient, low saddles can lead to knee injury.

The **saddle horizontal position** is set to give the most comfortable position for pedalling. The nose of the saddle should be about 5 cm (2 inches) behind a line passing vertically through the bottom bracket (1 in fig 1.1), but slight adjustments can make a lot of difference to comfort.

Saddle tilt also has an important effect on comfort, particularly

Figure 1.4
Checking saddle height

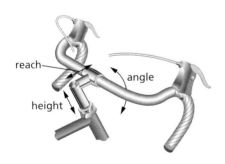

Figure 1.5
Handlebar adjustments

when riding longer distances. Most men prefer the nose slightly higher than the back, but for women the reverse is usually true and the saddle should tilt slightly downwards.

Next set the **handlebar height** (Figure 1.5), which should be about the same height as the top of the saddle. Slower or less supple riders may prefer the handlebars slightly higher than this, whilst a lower position can aid sprinting.

When adjusting the saddle height or handlebar height, if less than 5 cm (2 inches) of the seatpin or handlebar stem is left in the frame (there is usually a warning mark), the frame size is too small. Such a position is dangerous.

The **handlebar angle** is also important. Straight handlebars should be flat or sloping downwards a little towards the rider, and bar ends on ATB and hybrid bikes should be inclined a little more. Dropped handlebars should be set so that the top of the handlebars is horizontal.

The **handlebar reach**, in conjunction with the frame **top tube length** (30 in fig 1.1), also affects riding comfort by determining how easily you can hold the handlebars. With dropped handlebars, if you place your elbow against the front of the saddle, your fingertips should just be able to touch the middle of the handlebars (Figure 1.6). With straight handlebars, there is no such rule of thumb. Adjustable

7

stems are available for some bikes, but generally, changing handlebar reach requires the replacement of the handlebar stem. Women and very short or very tall men may find it difficult to achieve a comfortable saddle-to-handlebar distance on some cycles, even though the frames are nominally the correct size; in this case you should pay particular attention to choosing a frame with a top tube of suitable length. You should experiment with all the variables for the saddle and handlebar positions until you achieve the most comfortable ride.

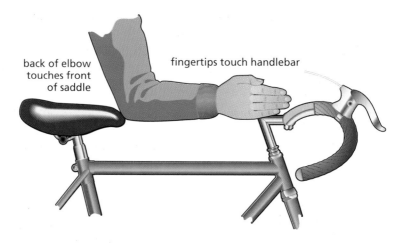

back of elbow touches front of saddle

fingertips touch handlebar

Figure 1.6
Checking handlebar reach

Brakes

The adjustments so far are, within reasonable limits, primarily concerned with comfort and efficiency. The ability to operate the brakes, however, is essential to safety. The correct positioning of the handlebars is an important factor in this, but the **brake levers** can also be moved along the handlebars and rotated around them.

Determining the best position for the brake levers is easiest with straight handlebars. There is usually only one hand position on the bars, and the brake levers should be adjacent to this, angled so that they are within comfortable reach of the fingers when lifted naturally. Keep brake levers as far as is practical towards the end of the handlebars, to maximise stability when braking.

With dropped handlebars, the situation is a little more complicated as there are several ways to hold the bars. The levers should be placed so that they can be operated from either below, on the drops, or above, from the top of the bars. Chapter 2 will explain more about the correct ways to operate these levers. Because most people make little use of the drops, the placing of the levers should normally favour the position which permits the easiest operation from above. You should be able to slide your hands smoothly and quickly forward from the top of the bars onto the brake levers, the tops of which should be at a similar height to the bars. A common error is to place the levers too low.

As with other handlebars, the angle of the levers on dropped handlebars should be set so that they can be operated comfortably. It is common for the levers to be turned outwards slightly.

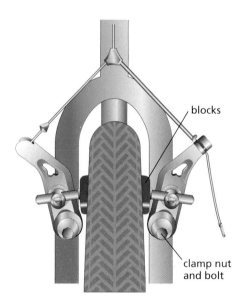

Whatever type of handlebar you have, check that the left lever operates the rear brake and the right lever operates the front brake.

The **brakes** themselves (Figure 1.7) need regular attention, as the blocks wear and the cables stretch. The **brake blocks** should be set so that whilst they normally clear the wheel rims, they come into operation with only a small movement of the levers, and the ends of the levers do not touch the handlebars, even when braking hard.

blocks

clamp nut and bolt

Figure 1.7
The brakes

A released clearance of 2 mm (0.08 inch) between each block and the rim is about right. With new blocks, this clearance should be set with the clamp nut and bolt (a 'third hand' tool is useful for this); thereafter, the barrel adjuster can be used to compensate for wear. If either wheel will not spin freely with such close adjustment, and if this cannot be corrected by slightly turning the whole brake mechanism, either the hub cones are loose or the wheel is out of true.

Always ensure that the brake blocks are set over the rims to give the greatest area of contact without touching the tyre wall at either end. If the shoe holding any block is open-ended, check that this points towards the back of the bike or the block may be dislodged during use. Sometimes, brake blocks squeal in use, which is not only embarrassing but also results in decreased stopping power; toeing the blocks in a little towards the front of the bike can help to overcome this. New blocks are best worn in by being used on a wet day. Make sure that you use the correct type of block for your rims: rubber or composition for alloy rims, leather-faced for steel.

The **brake cables** bear considerable strain and must be inspected frequently, particularly the end-nipples, which are hidden inside the brake levers. This is where most cables fray and then break. A little grease here can prolong life, whilst greasing the cable wire inside the outer sleeves also reduces friction and wear. If you ever brake hard in an emergency, or feel a lever moving more than normal, examine the cable for damage straight away.

Gears

Good gears are one of the most important assets a cycle can have if your cycling is to be pleasurable. Gears match the power output of the rider to the energy requirements of the cycle, which will vary with gradient and acceleration; this means you can achieve maximum efficiency with least effort. In Britain gears are specified in inches, and equate to the diameter of a fixed wheel that would cover the same distance per turn of the pedals – i.e., a gear of 40 inches is equivalent to pedalling a wheel of 40 inches diameter. On the Continent, the gear development is used, which is the distance a cycle actually travels per turn of the pedals. Hence a 40-inch gear is equivalent to a development of 3.2 metres.

A good range of gears is more important that the total number; some proprietary machines have their multiple gears very closely spaced. A bottom gear of 35–40 inches (2.8–3.2 m) and a top gear of about 90 inches (7.2 m) is suitable for riding in town traffic and up the hills encountered in most areas. However, to be able to tackle the really steep hills in some localities, a bottom gear of around 25 inches (2.0 m) is desirable. With a gear of this size it is possible to mount hills as steep as 40%, which is as steep as you will find on tarmac roads.

There are two types of gear mechanism: hub and derailleur. Hub gears are a little easier to use, more robust and need less attention, but are very difficult to service when they do go wrong. Three-speed hub gears provide too little range for most purposes, but versions with five or more speeds can be practical for utility riding or limited touring.

Derailleur gears are the most versatile, being the easiest to adapt to your particular requirements. They are available in combinations from 5 to 21 speeds or more. In most cases two gear mechanisms are used: a front changer which selects between chainwheels, and a rear changer which operates on the freewheel. Gear changing requires more skill, but this is not difficult to acquire, especially with indexed gears which, like hub gears, have pre-set lever positions for the rear changer. Further differences between hub and derailleur gears will be discussed in the next chapter.

With derailleurs of ten or more speeds, there are different theories and practices on how subsequent gears should be arranged. Probably the simplest is the sequential system, whereby you change through all the rear sprockets with one chainwheel before you change through the same sprockets with the others, but this only really works well when there is a big difference of size between chainwheels, with little overlap of gear ratios. This system has the big advantage that when you come to a sudden steep hill, you simply throw the front changer lever fully forward and you are immediately in a much lower gear.

The other common gear arrangement is to change alternately between rear and front changers to achieve a more evenly-spaced set of gears. With triple-chainwheel systems, the middle chainwheel is frequently used for normal riding whilst the two others effectively provide over- and under-drive for less frequently encountered conditions.

Correct adjustment of the gears is important for safety. Gear changing in traffic must be quick and precise; it is no place to stall or for gears to jump too far. Ensure that you can engage all usable gears easily and reliably without the chain falling off. For derailleur systems with multiple chainwheels there is usually an overlap of gears, and some of these cannot be used without the chain rubbing unsatisfactorily.

To adjust derailleur gears, you have to alter the top and bottom limit stops of the front and rear changers; there is an additional adjustment with indexed gears to synchronise the indexing. Hub gears vary, and should be adjusted in accordance with the manufacturer's instructions. In all cases, initial adjustments can be made with the cycle stationary and inverted, but some slight readjustment will usually be necessary to compensate for the greater forces present when pedalling.

Transmission

Moving parts benefit from cleaning and lubrication. The rule is little and often, but do keep lubricant away from brake blocks and gear levers. For efficiency and ease of gear changing, it is particularly important that the **transmission system** be kept in good condition. The chain gets rough treatment and should be re-lubricated each time it gets wet, and checked for wear every couple of months. To do this, pull the chain away from the front of the largest chainwheel with your hand; if it will move more than the height of a tooth, it has stretched too far and needs replacing (Figure 1.8). You may also need to replace the freewheel sprockets, as old sprockets and new chains do not always work well together.

Figure 1.8
Checking for chain wear

A further transmission system check is for play around the
bottom bracket (1 in fig 1.1). Grasp each pedal in turn and try
to rock it from side to side. Any significant movement means a
loose pedal, crank or bottom bracket. Then spin the pedals and
cranks backwards. Any great opposition may indicate an
overtight bearing.

Headset

A similar check for correct tightness should be made of the
headset. The handlebars should be able to turn with no apparent
friction, yet not be so loose that the bearings jar. With the front
brake held on, rock the cycle back and forth. Movement should
be restricted to that caused by the give of the tyres, and there
should be no noticeable movement between the front forks and
frame. A tight or a loose headset will lead to steering difficulties
and perhaps a dangerous wobble at speed. It will also result in
excessive wear of the headset cups and bearings.

Tyres

The last important check is of the **tyres**. Worn tyres are likely to
puncture more easily, whilst a smooth tread can be slippery in
the wet. (Some cycle tyres are smooth when new, but these are
really for racing, not general use.) It is important, too, that tyres
are inflated to the correct pressure. Most people would recognise

the dangers from explosion of over-inflated tyres, but few realise that under-inflating makes cycle control more difficult. Low pressures may also lead to reduced tyre life, increased risk of punctures and rim damage.

The majority of people considerably under-inflate their tyres; the only way of really being sure of the pressure is to buy a simple pressure gauge. The maximum tyre pressure should be printed on the tyre wall; for modern hybrid and sports cycle tyres, this will usually be 5–6 bar (70–90 pounds per square inch – psi). Although the maximum pressure should not be exceeded, the greater the pressure the more efficient will be your cycling on-road.

2 — Basic cycling skills

CHAPTER

Good cycling is a skill, make no mistake about it, but is easy to achieve given the right approach and some practice. It is worrying that too few cyclists bother to take that much trouble. One of the keys to safe cycling is that machine and rider operate as one: you should master the control of your bike so well that it becomes automatic, leaving you to give your full attention to the traffic and other hazards, or even to enjoy the countryside. Good control is efficient and satisfying, with all manoeuvres carried out smoothly, silently and purposefully. It is no coincidence that a good cyclist remains relaxed and does not suffer from road strain. It is also likely that most other road users will give you less trouble if they can see that you are a 'professional' who is in control.

The following skills start with the most basic, but even with these there are many regular cyclists who could benefit from improving their performance. Plenty of practice in these techniques is essential, and is best acquired away from traffic, on a quiet road or in a playground or similar open space. A few more advanced skills, such as steep hill climbing, are also covered in this chapter.

Balance and steering

Clearly a cyclist must have good balance, but this is not as simple as it seems – there is more to balancing than being able to keep upright. However, if you are new to cycling, this is the first skill to master.

Choose somewhere with a slight downhill slope and a good surface. Sit astride your machine, and with one foot on its pedal – in Britain, usually the right – push off. Fix your eyes on some point in the distance (not the ground just in front of you) and steer towards it. You should hold the handlebars close to the brake levers so that you can stop when you need to. Try not to be tense – control of any machine is always much easier if you are relaxed. Push the pedal foot down and, as you move off, position the other foot on its pedal. As you turn the pedals more quickly, you will find that steering becomes easier, but for really good balance you need to master the art of riding slowly. This requires practice.

As you ride, you should aim to steer as straight a course as possible. You should react to any tendency to go off course by subtly shifting your weight towards the opposite side. However, the correction needed is very small, and should not be overdone. Steering straight is accomplished by balance, which is aided by a smooth pedalling action. Keep your upper body still and do not attempt to turn the handlebars. Follow a straight line marked on the surface or some natural mark to perfect this. A good cyclist will wobble less than 2.5 cm (1 inch).

Pedalling

Pedalling should always be carried out with the ball of your foot, never with the instep. This is the most efficient pedalling position, and it is easier to achieve if you use toe clips or clipless pedals. These enable you to pull a pedal up as well as to push it down, and can increase pedalling efficiency by up to 50%. The use of toe clips and clipless pedals is described further in Chapter 13.

Another important rule of pedalling is to 'ankle' the pedals round: do not simply push them down. This means pivoting the foot at the ankle so that the toe is pointed slightly upwards at the top of the stroke and downwards at the bottom. In this way you should aim to apply pressure to each pedal with your foot for about three-quarters of its circle of travel (Figure 2.1).

Figure 2.1
Pedalling position and ankling

Acquiring a good pedalling style is important, and will help dispel the myth that cycling is hard work.

Holding the handlebars

Straight handlebars may have only one position for holding. Grip them firmly, but not too rigidly, and ensure that you can move your hands easily to apply the brake levers. Near hazards, you should keep your hands over the brake levers, ready to apply them.

Bar ends provide some straight handlebars with one or more alternative holding positions, which are similar to the upper positions of dropped handlebars, as described below. Always ensure that you can move easily from bar ends to the brake levers; extension levers (see page 186) may help.

There are four ways to hold dropped handlebars, and you should be able to move between these positions easily and without wobbling (Figure 2.2). The first thing to realise is that,

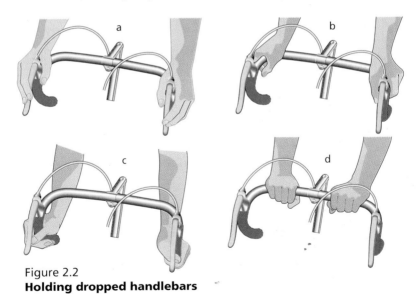

Figure 2.2
Holding dropped handlebars

a   normal position in traffic
b   relaxed position away from hazards
c   position against a strong headwind
d   alternative position for quiet roads

contrary to popular opinion, you will not often use the 'dropped' position (Figure 2.2c), unless you wish to cycle as a sport, riding as fast as possible on roads where good speeds can be maintained, in which case this is the most efficient position in terms of minimising wind resistance. In general, though, the dropped position is the least comfortable and generally the least practical in traffic. Nevertheless, the position can be useful when confronted by a strong headwind, so you should practise it.

The normal position for town riding, or for any other occasion when you may need to brake quickly, is to hold the tops of the brake levers with the thumb on one side and the fingers on the other (Figure 2.2a). The brakes are usually applied with the hands remaining in this position and the fingers reaching out for the levers about half-way down. This is a powerful braking position as the arms are straight, braced by the brake levers, and act to stop your body moving forward. With this posture you are least likely to be thrown over the handlebars when braking sharply. However, people with small or weak hands may not be able to do this easily (although smaller brake levers are available) and will need to brake from the drops. If this applies to you, always remember to allow extra braking time for the movement from top to drops – or you may find it easier to use straight handlebars.

The usual way to hold dropped handlebars when there are no hazards is to grasp them on top, just back from the brake levers where the bars run parallel to the direction of motion (Figure 2.2b). You should be able to slide from here to the levers smoothly and quickly.

The last position (Figure 2.2d) is used as an alternative when riding longer distances, in order to relieve pressure on the hands. Here, the straight section of the handlebars either side of the stem is grasped with the fingers in front and the thumb behind. This position is the slowest for moving to the brakes, so you should move back to one of the others at the slightest hint of a hazard. However, it is a good position to use while you perfect your balance, as the hands are closest together and the bike is at its least stable.

Braking

Braking should be practised whatever type of handlebars you use. You should be able to move your hands quickly to the levers and to apply them with just the right amount of force to slow down or stop in the distance required. This means that you must get to know the 'feel' of your brakes, and you must keep them adjusted so that this feel remains constant over time. Practise applying different amounts of force to the levers, and learn the total distances before you are brought to a halt, as well as the initial distances before the brakes have any significant effect. It is particularly important to practise this under both dry and wet conditions, as there will be a very marked difference between the two distances when the wheel rims and road are wet.

There is another element that must be included in the total stopping distance that has nothing to do with the brakes, but which can be significant. This is the reaction time – the distance you travel between seeing an incident which requires you to brake and responding to it. Reaction time will vary between about a second and 2.5 seconds, depending upon how alert you are; and at 32 km/h (20 mph) you will cover nearly 23 metres (75 feet) in 2.5 seconds!

Table 2.1 shows typical total braking distances of cycles for extreme states of weather and rider on roads with different gradients. Notice how much greater the distances become under imperfect conditions. All distances relate to alloy-wheel cycles; in wet weather, steel-wheeled machines can take up to twice as far to stop.

You should also learn the difference in effect between the front and rear brakes. Getting to know the action of each brake on its own at an early stage under controlled conditions could prove useful should one of the brake cables snap. By far the greatest amount of stopping power comes from the front brake, but if this is used too violently, the cycle will pivot on the front wheel and you will be thrown over the handlebars. The rear brake is most useful to fine-tune your speed on gradual descents and in traffic.

Table 2.1
Total stopping distance on a cycle

	16 km/h (10 mph)	24 km/h (15 mph)	32 km/h (20 mph)	40 km/h (25 mph)
Gradient: 0%, level				
Dry and alert	6 m (20 ft)	11 m (36 ft)	17 m (56 ft)	24 m (79 ft)
Wet and tired	15 m (49 ft)	27 m (89 ft)	41 m (134 ft)	57 m (187 ft)
Gradient: 5%, down				
Dry and alert	6 m (20 ft)	11 m (36 ft)	18 m (59 ft)	25 m (82 ft)
Wet and tired	17 m (56 ft)	30 m (98 ft)	47 m (154 ft)	67 m (220 ft)
Gradient: 10%, down				
Dry and alert	7 m (23 ft)	12 m (39 ft)	19 m (62 ft)	27 m (89 ft)
Wet and tired	20 m (66 ft)	37 m (121 ft)	58 m (190 ft)	84 m (276 ft)

If you need to brake at all quickly, you need to apply both brakes. For maximum efficiency and safety, 75% of the braking power should be applied to the front brake and 25% to the rear on a firm, dry road. In the wet, it is important to modify this to 50:50. Practise applying the rear brake a fraction of a second before the front until this becomes second nature every time. As far as possible, only brake when steering straight.

Even if you do use both brakes, braking too rapidly can still be dangerous as one or both wheels may lock. Judging when this may occur will take time. Meanwhile, don't try braking more hastily than you know is safe unless you really have no choice.

Accurate steering

Although you should by now be able to steer straight, it is also important to be able to steer accurately, placing your wheels precisely where you want them in order to avoid pot-holes and stones. Fortunately, this can be achieved quite easily, as our normal stereoscopic vision has the remarkable ability to be able to judge whether an object lies straight ahead to an accuracy of better than 1°.

To practise accurate steering, mark two parallel chalk lines on the ground about 30 cm (12 inches) long and 8 cm (3 inches) apart. Ride between the lines repeatedly until neither the front nor the rear wheel touches them at normal riding speed (Figure 2.3). This is most easily judged by a friend standing nearby. As soon as you have mastered this, decrease the spacing to 5 cm (2 inches) and then to 2.5 cm (1 inch). When you can achieve this accuracy consistently, you will be an important step closer to harmonising the movements of bike and body.

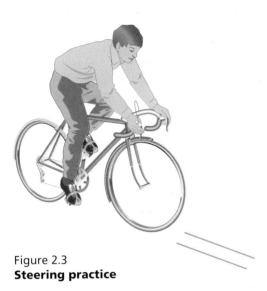

Figure 2.3
Steering practice

Control with one hand

Up to now you have practised maintaining good balance while looking ahead and with both hands on the handlebars. However, it is also important for you to be able to control your machine with only one hand and without looking where you are going! You need this skill to be able to look behind and then to signal before manoeuvring.

Lift each hand in turn from the handlebars while riding straight ahead: first by just a little, and then move it well away to the side of your body. You will soon realise that the other hand must compensate for the imbalance by pressing a little harder on the handlebar and at a slightly different angle. Move the free hand to and from the handlebars until you make this adjustment easily.

Signalling

Now focus on lifting the free arm to give a right- or left-turn signal as appropriate. Always signal with the full arm straight out and fingers pointed so that there can be no doubt whatsoever about your intentions (Figure 2.4). Also practise the slowing-down or stopping signal, in which the right arm moves between the body and a position 45° to the horizontal. You will notice that the compensation necessary by the other arm is slightly different in each case.

The straight-ahead signal, also shown in Figure 2.4, is used to give information about your intentions to someone directing traffic, such as a police officer.

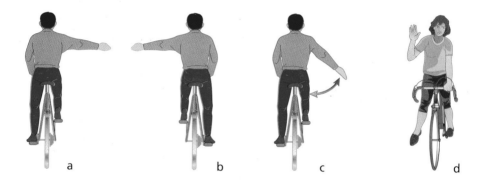

a   b   c   d

Figure 2.4
Signalling

a   intention to move or turn right
b   intention to move or turn left
c   slowing down or stopping
d   intention to go ahead

Looking behind

Once you are reasonably confident about keeping a straight course with only one hand, practise looking behind. This is the most difficult action to perfect in terms of keeping the bike

Figure 2.5
Looking behind

travelling in a straight line. Practise it first with both hands on the handlebars – the normal position in traffic – and then lower the hand on the side over which you are looking behind (Figure 2.5). The latter manoeuvre allows a greater turn and hence better visibility of what is happening behind, but takes longer so is best not done on busy roads.

Even with both hands on the handlebars, you will soon realise that most of the steering control now comes from the hand on the 'blind' side. The other hand is essentially for steadying. Whilst in the majority of instances you will wish to look over your right shoulder, practise looking over the left shoulder, too, as this can sometimes be very useful.

Avoiding obstacles

Having carefully acquired the skill of riding as straight as possible, it is now time to learn how not to! You may, for example, need to avoid pot-holes and other obstacles.

Place three small objects or chalk marks on the surface of the ground, 4 metres (13 feet) apart in a straight line. Weave between them, passing alternately to the left and to the right (Figure 2.6). You should aim to veer as little as possible from the straight line – swerving in traffic could put you into the path of following vehicles.

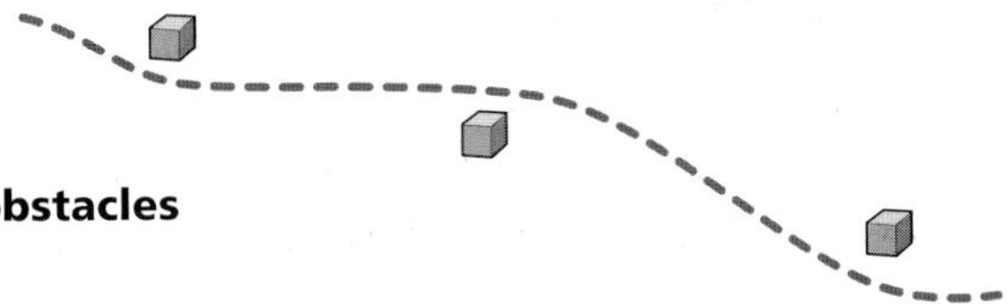

Figure 2.6
Practising avoiding obstacles

Having succeeded in avoiding obstacles 4 metres (13 feet) apart, decrease the spacing, in stages, to about 0.5 metres (1.5 feet or so). As the spacing reduces, you will find that it will not be possible to make the rear wheel follow the front; this does not matter too much, as you are more vulnerable to toppling over from deflection of the front wheel by an obstacle than from deflection of the back. Also, whilst you should be able to negotiate the first spacings reasonably quickly, as spacing decreases, so must your speed.

For isolated or widely-spaced small obstacles, it is possible with some practice to keep both the body and handlebars moving in virtually a straight line while the cycle wheels move from side to side. As the wheels are much narrower than the rider, this can result in virtually no deflection of the cycle and cyclist's combined path. To achieve this, approach a single object in a straight line until you are very close. Then turn the handlebars suddenly – just a little – so that your front wheel misses the object, but without first leaning in the same direction as you would normally. Your body will start to fall in the opposite direction, but you counter this by steering back towards that side as soon as your front wheel is past the object. You will need to oversteer somewhat in order to compensate for the unusual body angle, but you then straighten both handlebars and body to continue on your original course (Figure 2.7). There is no doubt that this technique needs practice, for you will need to make movements which at first seem unnatural. Having learnt it, though, you will not only be able to avoid holes and stones, but you will also be able to make quick turns more easily in an emergency.

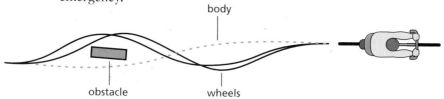

Figure 2.7
Advanced obstacle avoidance

Turning

Steering control can now be developed further as you practise making turns. In practice, for many changes of direction, 'turning' is the wrong term to use, as the front wheel is only turned when you want to follow tight corners or when travelling very slowly. At other times the handlebars remain almost straight and the cycle moves around a bend by being leaned in that direction in order to counteract the centrifugal force on the wheels. The degree of lean necessary is proportional to both the tightness of the turn and to your speed. Practise making turns of increasing tightness and at increased speed. You will soon find that you make the correct amount of lean automatically. Don't overdo the leaning, particularly if the surface is not firm, or your wheels may slip from under you. It is not advisable to find the limiting angle by trial and error!

The tightest turn that you will commonly make is the left turn at a crossroads. Find such a junction on a quiet road and notice how the kerb is radiused around the corner. You should be able to approach the corner and ride around it while keeping your rear wheel parallel to the kerb all the time (Figure 2.8). The front wheel will inevitably turn more widely at normal speed, and you should learn the exact amount of oversteering necessary. This practice becomes even more important if you ride a tandem

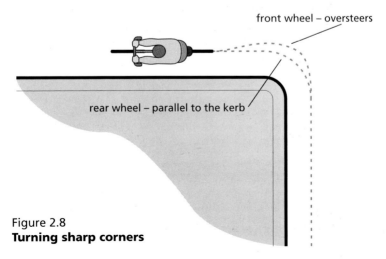

front wheel – oversteers

rear wheel – parallel to the kerb

Figure 2.8
Turning sharp corners

or pull a trailer, as the amount of oversteering is then more significant. Turning too widely – a common fault – may put you in danger from traffic.

Practise making the turn at different distances from the kerb where the camber (arch) of the road – and hence the kind of control necessary – may differ. Occasionally, you will encounter more acute angles, and you should practise turning as sharply as you can to both the left and right.

U-turns

A useful extension of your turning practice is to see how tight a U-turn you can manage. You should certainly be able to U-turn within a normal two-lane road. Safe U-turning requires low speed, a low gear to help you keep balance, a generally upright position and the ability to stay relaxed. Take particular care if your feet (or toe clips) can touch the front mudguard as this could lock you into the turn, resulting in a fall. In such cases a shunting movement of the pedals, to keep them clear of the front wheel, is necessary.

Listening

An essential skill for understanding what's going on around you is listening. Here the unencumbered cyclist has an important advantage over most other drivers, as traffic noises are considerably muted inside a motor vehicle. Your ears should be active all the time, unscrambling the background din for any noise that could mean danger. You will soon get to know the obvious sounds, such as the screeching of brakes or fierce acceleration, but detecting the change in pitch of a car engine as the driver decides to pull in behind you or to come out across your path will require some practice.

Good hearing is vital for a cyclist. If you wear a hat, keep it clear of your ears, and on no account should you listen to audio equipment while you are cycling.

Changing gear

No mention has yet been made of changing gear, but this ability is essential, both on hills and in traffic. The technique for changing gear depends on whether you have hub or derailleur gears.

Hub gears can be changed when you are freewheeling or stationary, but not when you are applying pressure to the pedals. This has both advantages and drawbacks. You do not have to think about changing down when you are approaching traffic lights, or anywhere else where you might have to stop, because you can do so after stopping (although it is still good practice to anticipate a change). On the other hand, you must change down before hills in order not to lose too much momentum while you ease off pedalling.

To change hub gears, simply move the lever at the same time as you briefly stop pedalling. In some cases rotating the pedals backwards slightly can make for an easier change. Five-speed hub gears sometimes require the operation of two levers, but in all cases there are quite definite notches for the levers for each gear, and changing should be accurate so long as the gear has been set up correctly.

In contrast, derailleur gears can only be changed when you are pedalling, which means that you must anticipate occasions when you might have to stop and would need to be in a lower gear. However, you will not lose too much momentum changing down to climb hills. With 10 or more speeds, there is a second lever to change the chainwheel, in addition to that for changing the freewheel sprocket.

The development of indexed gears has made gear changing on derailleur-equipped cycles easier for many people. Like a hub gear, the rear gear lever has pre-determined positions for each gear. To change gear, you continue to pedal, but ease up a little on the pressure applied. This will decrease the tension in the chain and make for an easier and quieter change. Then simply click the gear lever between positions. If the gears have been correctly adjusted, changing of the rear sprockets should be accurate.

Non-indexed gear levers are held in the various positions merely by friction and have no pre-determined positions for each gear. Some indexed levers can be set to friction mode by means of a small switch at the back of the lever; you should learn to use them in this way as a back-up against any sudden malfunctioning of the index mechanism. This can occur when mud or debris enters the gear mechanism or when a cable stretches. In addition, many cyclists prefer the quicker gear changing that friction changing can offer – an advantage in traffic.

Because of the need to determine the correct lever position interactively, gear changing with friction levers requires the use of your ears as well as your hands and feet! Reduce pedalling pressure and move the gear lever until you have gone just beyond the desired gear – this produces the fastest change – and then bring it back slightly as the chain settles into place, finely adjusting for minimum noise in the transmission system. Don't stay in a noisy gear: it is inefficient and accelerates chain wear.

Sometimes when changing gear on the rear sprockets you will also have to slightly readjust the front changer, and vice versa, because the overall chain line will alter. With practice, you will be able to achieve this quickly each time, and you will learn to recognise by feel the gear you have reached without looking down.

Front gear levers are also available in both indexed and friction types. To change chainwheels, move the lever until the chain moves across, and then bring it back a little so that the changer is clear of the chain. You should operate both the front and rear levers with the same hand, usually the right. Although a little awkward at first, this method allows you to move both levers simultaneously if necessary, and you can also make any compensatory adjustments with the other lever more quickly. Fast and accurate gear changing is important in traffic.

When changing to a lower gear, you should be able to do it by one rear sprocket at a time, whatever your gearing system. When changing to a higher gear, though, it is not unusual to jump two or more sprockets per change, especially on non-indexed mechanisms. This is not normally important, but can be a nuisance when ascending hills, when fine gear changes are essential. However, as the gradient gets easier it is not difficult to pedal in a lower gear than ideal for what will usually be only a short time. Alternatively, you can compensate for a change to too high a gear by changing immediately back to a lower one.

The hardest gear change to make smoothly is when you are only part way up a long hill and the gradient has eased just a little. It can then be difficult to reduce pressure on the pedals sufficiently for a smooth change, whilst riding in too low a gear would become increasingly tiring. In this case, pedal faster than usual over a short distance in order to achieve sufficient additional momentum to reduce pedal pressure so that you can change gear without your speed falling to less than that at which you started. A similar technique can be used to change to a larger chainwheel.

Get to know your own gears, and practise changing them until you can select any new gear quickly, smoothly and quietly.

Hill climbing

Climbing hills need not be hard work, but for many cyclists the use of inadequate gears or the wrong technique certainly make it so. Tackled properly, almost any hill can be climbed more easily by riding than by dismounting and pushing.

As you approach a hill, start to change to a lower gear as soon as you feel that your normal pedalling rate (known as 'cadence': see page 34) is beginning to decrease. By far the commonest fault amongst cyclists in hill climbing is changing gear too late, by which time they are more exhausted than is necessary. With practice you should be able to change before your cadence decreases, in order to anticipate the loss of momentum which inevitably occurs during a gear change. Learn just how much momentum you do lose under differing circumstances and detect the increase in pedalling effort which precedes a reduction in pedalling speed; this is the correct time to change gear. Your aim should be to keep the pedals turning at the cadence which matches your maximum efficiency, at least until you have reached the bottom gear and can go no further.

If a hill is gradual, you should change down one gear at a time following the procedure detailed above. As the gradient slackens, change back to higher gears as soon as you can, to increase speed and maintain cadence. However, if a hill is steep, you will waste much less momentum if you change down several gears at a time. When the need to use a smaller chainring seems likely, be sure to change to this in good time, as it is more difficult to move the front changer under pressure than the rear. On sudden, severe hills, it is often best to go straight to a very low gear and then to change up slowly if you find that you have gone too far. If the latter is the case, pedal a bit faster while changing back up; to maintain the same cadence in this instance might reduce control and make balancing more difficult.

As you near the top of a steep hill, change back up again, although you may first find it more refreshing to pedal a short while in what would otherwise be too low a gear. This is particularly beneficial during a series of steep ups and downs, giving the leg muscles some chance to recuperate.

Once you reach the bottom gear, it will no longer be possible to maintain normal cadence, and your pedalling will slow down. At first you may feel that this is the point to get off and walk, but don't! Part of the skill in riding up steep hills is having the patience to ride up slowly. Although it may seem dreadfully slow compared with a preceding descent, it will still be faster than walking. It is at this time, if you are on a quiet road with little traffic, that you can look at your surroundings, which will take your mind off your speed, or lack of it. Before you realise it, you will be at the top.

There are two limiting factors which determine how steep a hill you can cycle up. The first is your ability to maintain balance, and the second is the tendency of the front wheel to lift off the ground on really steep climbs. Given suitable gears, the strength of the rider is less important, although regular hill climbing strengthens the calf muscles and makes the activity easier. At low speeds on steep gradients it is almost impossible to steer a straight line. Climbing can be made easier if you reduce the mean gradient by zigzagging across the road. Obviously, this can only be done if there is no traffic and you are sure that the way ahead is clear. With traffic, take care not to put yourself at risk by riding too irregular a course, although too great an effort to keep straight might mean that a following driver will not appreciate your difficulties and will give you too little clearance. To stop the front wheel lifting, throw your weight towards the front of the bicycle by crouching and keeping your head low, but only do this as much as is necessary, since steering will become more difficult.

If you are approaching an uphill after a downhill gradient where you were able to freewheel, make the most of the energy gained from the descent to help you on the way up (Figure 2.9). On the way down, select a high gear and start pedalling when the hill flattens out as soon as your freewheeling speed decreases to that matched by the selected gear. Then continue to pedal at your normal cadence while changing down again as necessary. This may seem like a lot of gear changing, but it is the most efficient way of riding. Too many cyclists wait until they have reached the very bottom of a descent before starting to pedal again, even braking when they should be pedalling, with the result that they need to supply much more energy for the new climb. Nearing the bottom of a hill, you should not normally brake to a speed less than that at which you can pedal, assuming, of course, that visibility and traffic conditions are favourable.

| check brakes | change up in gear to match speed | keep speed in check | start pedalling as hill flattens out | change down in gear as necessary to maintain cadence | recuperate before changing up after steep hills |

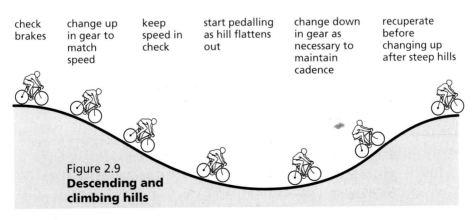

Figure 2.9
Descending and climbing hills

Notice that nowhere in the advice given so far has there been any mention of standing on the pedals to climb a hill. There is a good reason for this. Standing causes the cycle to lurch from side to side to counter the imbalance of the body. Although standing can enable you to transmit more power to the cycle, it is a much less efficient means of pedalling than the correct 'ankling' technique (see fig 2.1), as the force to turn the pedals is applied through a smaller angle of pedal movement and to only one side at a time. Selecting a lower gear, remaining seated and ankling the pedals is a much less tiring and more elegant way of riding.

There is, however, one circumstance when standing on the pedals can be useful. This is when you have to surmount a very short rise either when travelling fast on an otherwise level road (e.g., over a bridge), where a double gear change in quick succession would otherwise be necessary, or if you accidentally failed to change down sufficiently in advance and a further change would make you lose too much momentum, possibly putting you at risk in traffic.

Should you have to stop on a steep hill, restarting can be difficult even if you are in a low gear. Often you will not be able to gain your balance at the first attempt, but by pushing off again as soon as a foot lands back on the ground, you will have a little more momentum and you may then succeed. On really sharp slopes, a multiple push start might be necessary. In all cases, try to engage the second toe clip as you mount. You will probably not be able to stop your pedalling sufficiently in order to do this afterwards, and hill climbing is more strenuous without toe clips.

Many of the techniques in this section on hill climbing may not be needed, especially if your cycling is confined to towns, but you should practise them if the opportunity arises.

Descending hills

Going downhill is the time for a cyclist to rest the legs, but that is the only part of the body that can relax. Although climbing hills requires the most physical energy, it is generally descending a hill that requires the most mental energy and concentration.

You will be travelling faster, conditions around you will change more quickly, and the consequences of any fall will be more severe.

The first thing to do at the very beginning of a descent – any and every descent – is to check that your brakes still work! This is the only time during the descent that you will be able to stop without brakes with reasonable safety. If the descent is gradual, you can then release the brakes a little, but keep your hands over the levers, with the levers pulled such that the brake blocks are only just clear of the rims. The speed to which you can safely allow yourself to accelerate depends very much upon the nature of the road – its straightness, visibility, surface quality, the number of side roads and entrances, and the presence of other vehicles, moving or parked. **At no time should you ride faster than a speed at which you can safely and easily stop within the distance you can see to be clear.** To ensure this, curb your speed when necessary by applying the brakes continuously once the limiting speed has been reached.

Knowledge of how fast you can go under different circumstances is only gained through experience, and you should practise braking on different types of hill until you are confident about your bike's capabilities. Never assume that you can always brake a bit harder when you need to; the chances are that it is then that a brake cable will snap. In fact, to minimise cable wear, as well as to have something in reserve for genuine emergencies, you should always apply the brakes gradually, not suddenly.

If a hill is steep, keep your speed right down from the start so that it is well below that which might be safe on a gradual hill, or you may not be able to stop sufficiently quickly if you suddenly need to. On very steep hills, this can mean descending at a speed not much faster than that at which you would cycle up, and the braking force required may make your hands hurt. Take care not to weaken your hands by applying this sort of effort for too long.

A problem on long, steep hills is that the wheel rims get very hot and, in extreme cases, there is a risk of this causing an explosion of the inner tube. Although modern composition tubes are less prone to this danger than the older rubber types, care should be taken not to heat up the rims too much. One way to reduce the heat a little is to apply the brakes with a 'pumping' on-and-off action; another, where there is no traffic, is to zigzag slowly downwards in order to reduce the mean gradient. On the worst hills, stopping is advisable every so often to cool the rims, and to rest your hands. These considerations are particularly important with heavily-laden cycles and tandems, as weight is an important factor (which is why tandems are best fitted with an additional hub or disc brake).

Keeping a check of your speed is not the only important aspect of keeping your bike under control when descending hills. You should also be able to take over control with the pedals if necessary, for example, to outpace a dog or a car coming suddenly into your path. Many motorists considerably underestimate the speed of cycles on hills. You will learn later that it is often better to accelerate out of trouble than to slow down. To be able to resume pedalling quickly, you need to be in a gear which would give a pedalling speed closest to that at which you freewheel. You should therefore normally change up to a suitable gear at the start of a descent. The principal exception to this is if you are riding through a series of short, sharp hills, when excessive gear changing could be a nuisance.

Cadence and sprint speed

Cadence is defined as the number of times a cyclist turns the pedals in one minute. A steady, comfortable pedalling rhythm is essential for efficient cycling, whilst increasing one's cadence strengthens the leg muscles and enables more rapid acceleration. Increasing cadence also makes it easier to increase your sprint speed – the maximum speed you can attain over a short distance, such as through a roundabout.

Racing cyclists know well the benefits of having a high cadence, but there can also be important safety advantages for a town cyclist. Generally speaking, you are at your safest in traffic if you can move at a speed comparable to that of the other vehicles.

Increasing your cadence and sprint speed will allow you to achieve this more often, particularly where you would otherwise be vulnerable due to complex manoeuvring. It will also be easier to restart quickly in a low gear at traffic signals and roundabouts, and to get yourself out of trouble if you are on a potential collision course.

Increasing cadence and sprint speed are two of the most positive steps a cyclist can take to enhance safety. A good cadence to aim for is about 80, whilst a sprint speed of 32 km/h (20 mph) will enable you to tackle most traffic situations with ease.

To increase your cadence, select a gear lower than you would normally use for a given road and simply force yourself to pedal faster in order to maintain your usual speed. Gradually, your leg muscles will become accustomed to the higher rate and your cadence and strength will increase.

Collision avoidance techniques

A careful cyclist will aim not to get into situations which could result in a collision with anyone else; certainly, there are many situations in which potential crashes can easily be avoided. Watchfulness and anticipation are the primary collision avoidance techniques, and are all that should be necessary for the great majority of the time.

However, because a cyclist is so vulnerable to the actions of others, and there are many drivers on the roads today who do not appreciate the problems cyclists face, there may be times when you will have to react quickly to an error by someone else if you are to avoid injury. You may have to decide how to react in only a fraction of a second, and the precise action required will vary from situation to situation. None the less, there are certain last-moment collision avoidance techniques which you can learn and practise, to deal with a potential conflict.

There are three responses to an emergency:

- brake sharply;

- accelerate;

- change direction quickly.

The most instinctive response is to brake sharply, but this is often not the best thing to do. The problems with braking are: firstly, cycle brakes are poor; secondly, their sudden, sharp application is liable to lock a wheel or rip the cable – in either case you will probably go over the handlebars; thirdly, you end up stationary in the conflict zone itself, which is no good if a car is still coming towards you.

Braking is usually only the best way to avoid a collision if you are still some distance from it and you are reasonably confident of being able to stop well short, without toppling. If you do brake quickly, brake hard with the front brake but with normal severity at the back. As you brake, throw your weight backwards in the saddle, which will reduce the braking distance and improve your stability.

Often you can avoid a collision most easily by accelerating rapidly away from it. Aim to get away from the conflict zone as quickly as possible. Although motor vehicles are capable of much faster maximum speeds and acceleration rates than cyclists, it is surprising just how fast a cyclist can move when it really matters, particularly if a high cadence has been acquired. This is often sufficient to get you out of the way of a car which fails to give way at a roundabout or which looks likely not to stop when coming out of a side road. Developing the skill of judging the speed of other vehicles will allow you to decide if there is likely to be time to outpace someone. If so, just pedal like fury – there'll be no time to change gear!

Making a sudden change of direction is usually the best response to dangerous turning movements by cars at junctions. It can also be useful for avoiding pot-holes and other hazards, but these will be discussed more fully in Chapter 7. If a vehicle pulls out of a side road across your path but you are not sufficiently advanced to be able to accelerate out of the way, make a quick diversionary turn towards the offside of the car (Figure 2.10a). This, of course, will put you in some danger from any following traffic, but in practice whilst a driver may pull out without seeing a cyclist, this is less likely if another vehicle is coming. In any case, good observation on the part of the cyclist should suggest in advance that this situation might happen, leaving sufficient time to slow down and look behind. Holding the primary riding position, as will be described in Chapter 4, will mean that you are more likely to be seen, and that your avoiding manoeuvre need be less severe if you are not.

Less easily avoided is the situation when a car overtakes a cyclist and then suddenly pulls into the kerb to stop (Figure 2.10b). Sometimes drivers behave in this way just to get themselves out of a fast stream of traffic. Often the cyclist cannot match the car's deceleration; a further possible hazard is that the driver,

a   b

Figures 2.10a and 2.10b
Diversionary turns

having stopped, will open a door straight into your path. Maintaining a position away from the kerb will help to minimise the swerve that it may then be necessary to make into traffic.

A similar situation, and one of the commonest causes of collisions with cyclists, is when a car overtakes a cyclist and then turns left across the cyclist's path at a junction or entrance. If this happens so close to the junction that braking is not practicable (often you can detect the situation arising by the sound of the car slowing down as it overtakes, and you can then start to brake early), the only response is to make a tight left turn into the same side road in order to keep to the left of the car (Figure 2.11). Tight left turns are very hard to do and a little hazardous to practise. The idea is that the first movement you

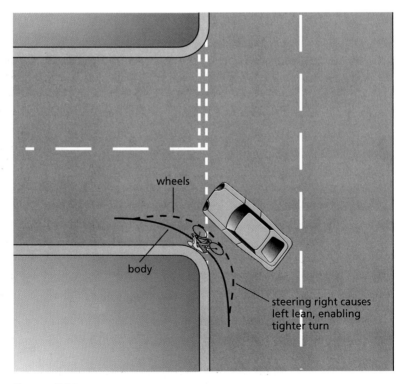

wheels

body

steering right causes left lean, enabling tighter turn

Figures 2.11
The quick left turn

make is to turn the handlebars *right*, towards the car. This throws the body to the left, and when, a split second later, the handlebars are turned left, the body is already leaning and the turn will be that much tighter. The same technique is applicable if a car from the opposite direction turns right across your path. In neither case is it wise to veer right instead of left, as that will take you towards the car, which could result in a head-on collision or you passing under a wheel – such crashes are likely to be fatal.

On occasions, a combination of two of the three avoidance techniques may be best, usually starting with braking, and then steering past an obstacle once you are going slow enough to do so, or accelerating again to respond to a change in a driver's behaviour.

Being prepared

For a skilled cyclist, crashes are very rare. None the less, despite all you do to avoid it, it is prudent to be prepared for a crash. In collision with something, or if the cycle slips, a cyclist is invariably thrown into the air, if only for a second or two. The greatest potential danger is that the head will hit something hard, such as the ground. By comparison, other injuries are relatively unimportant. Action to minimise or control injury requires great presence of mind, but it could help if you've thought about it beforehand.

In so much as you have any control over the orientation of your body, try to keep upright for as long as possible. This will lessen the chances of your body or head going under the wheels of another vehicle. Then look at your knees! The effect of this should be to turn your head inwards, which will minimise the likelihood of your skull hitting the road. If you are sufficiently alert to roll yourself up into a ball, so much the better.

Even if you have landed without any apparent serious injury, take your time getting back up – unless, of course, it seems likely that someone will drive into you. Move carefully, checking all over for injury, then sit still for a while to recover from the shock. It is unwise to carry on while still dazed. When you have recovered, check your bike over carefully for any signs of damage, looking particularly at the wheels, frame and brakes.

3 — Sharing the roads

A common reason given by people for not cycling is that sharing the roads with motor vehicles is too dangerous. Bikes and cars, it is thought, are incapable of mixing safely. From this follows the argument that to maximise their safety, cyclists should keep (or be kept) out of the way of motor traffic as much as possible.

In fact, nothing could be further from the truth. Cars and cycles can mix well, and they usually do. A considerable number of people cycle regularly in traffic with surprisingly little difficulty. As you will read in the chapter on cycle facilities (Chapter 10), no alternative to the general road network has yet been devised which is as safe or advantageous overall for cycling.

Cycling safely on the roads is not simply a matter of luck, nor does it depend solely upon the behaviour of the drivers of motor vehicles, although cyclists are certainly always vulnerable to the actions of others. Safe cycling is also a matter of adopting sensible techniques, for in practice, most drivers co-operate with cyclists who follow the rules of the road in a confident and disciplined manner.

Feeling at ease on the roads is largely a matter of gaining confidence, whereas being safe requires both expert control of your machine, and also the ability to 'read' the road and to predict and respond to the behaviour of others. Other sections of this book deal in detail with developing these skills.

Another equally important aspect of road sharing is the development of psychological skills – understanding why other drivers behave in the way they do, and seeking to achieve a helpful relationship with them.

Attitude

Having the right attitude towards your cycling and others is extremely important if you are to cycle well and safely. Without the correct frame of mind – having an awareness both of your rights and responsibilities – you will give yourself unnecessary problems by encouraging others to make mistakes or by annoying them needlessly. Research suggests that cyclists who are tolerant to others have a significantly lower risk of conflict.

The first thing to realise is that very few drivers are deliberately aggressive; they are simply intent, like you, on getting from one place to another with the minimum of trouble. Drivers hardly ever choose to have a collision with a cyclist. Having said that, people often do stupid things. Probably the most common driver error is impatience. You need to recognise that the training of motorists is often inadequate, with the emphasis more on passing the driving test than on acquiring safe driving skills. It is rare indeed for motorists to be taught anything about sharing the roads with non-motorised traffic, or anything about the difficulties faced by people such as cyclists. If you study this book well, you will achieve a greater level of skill and understanding than the average motorist – or the average cyclist for that matter.

It is also true that some aspects of modern vehicle design increase the difficulties motorists have in controlling their vehicles safely on all-traffic roads. The amount of power under a driver's command is several times greater than only a few years ago. Features such as the fast rates of acceleration and braking now possible with even an average family saloon encourage some drivers to travel at speeds greater than those at which they are competent, and tempt them to take more risks because it is now easier for them to get *themselves* out of trouble.

Road design, too, can cause problems for drivers. Many motorists find busy roundabouts and complex intersections as intimidating and difficult to use as do many cyclists. So much of their attention is devoted to finding the correct route and looking out for others who might hit them that there often isn't a lot of attention left to spot a cyclist. Drivers may also be pressured by other traffic into making quick decisions on limited information.

With both vehicle and road design, engineering improvements can improve safety as well as convenience, but some drivers abuse these advantages without necessarily thinking of the consequences for others. As a cyclist, you need to be aware of all these limitations of drivers and to allow for them.

Do not let yourself be annoyed by others, however stupid their actions. This will take your attention from the road and could lead you from a near miss to a certain hit. Develop the ability to curse and then forget. One of the great advantages of cycling is that the physical effort involved can help to dispel anger and frustration quickly and harmlessly. The same doesn't apply to someone sitting motionless in a car, who may continue to resent some thoughtless action of yours long after you have forgotten it.

Likewise, don't retaliate with abuse or a siren. You may cause greater trouble for the next cyclist the driver meets. Of course, if someone has acted aggressively towards you with intent, note the registration number and make a report to the police, although the chances of proceedings following are slim unless there is a witness.

Riding around with a feeling of superiority to others is also foolish. A halo offers no protection against the bad driving of others; indeed, bad driving may even be encouraged by such a 'holier-than-thou' attitude on the part of the cyclist.

A sensible attitude to adopt when cycling is that you are an equal to all others on the road. Do not be submissive to others, and exert your rights if this does not put you into undue danger. Be equally prepared, however, to yield to the rights of others and to show tolerance and understanding of the difficulties that all road users have. You should also appreciate that even a cyclist is capable of causing injury or nuisance to others.

Curiously, the biggest mistake made by many cyclists is that they are too submissive when sharing the roads, somehow feeling that they must always allow priority to motor vehicles. It is precisely this attitude that causes many of their difficulties in traffic. You need to appreciate that, as a cyclist, you have as much right as any other to be on the road, with as much right to an easy journey. Although a lack of caution is certainly unwise, so is a lack of confidence. If you keep giving way or hesitate when the right of way is yours, you will not only get nowhere fast, but the resulting confusion may well put you more at risk than if you'd been more assertive.

Courtesy on the roads has unfortunately diminished considerably in recent years, yet it is an essential ingredient for safety. Try to show courtesy and patience when you can, and give a brief 'thank you' signal if someone does you a kindness. It is remarkable the goodwill that this can generate.

Judgement

Good judgement of road conditions and of the behaviour of others is important if you are to cycle positively and confidently. The ability to make wise judgements more consistently gives the adult cyclist an important advantage over a child, who cannot be expected to discriminate so reliably, and who therefore needs to ride more submissively. Adults should not need to do this.

Judgement is largely a matter of experience and is closely related to observation, which will be discussed more fully in Chapter 4. But much can be learned simply by looking critically at the actions of others, both motorists and cyclists.

Go to a busy road junction, preferably one without traffic signals – a simple give way junction or a roundabout is a good place. Watch closely how drivers behave. Whilst you can never recognise for sure a good driver – which is why any judgement needs to have an adequate margin for error – there are certain tell-tale indicators of poor driving. Close overtaking, weaving and the failure to give way to others are obvious faults. Much bad driving is noisy, with fierce braking and acceleration, inappropriate speed, and impatient turning. Cars with unnecessary embellishments and souped-up engines can indicate aggressiveness on the part of their drivers, but don't assume that all bad driving is aggressive. Many drivers are simply lazy, tired or incompetent and react too slowly. Identify carefully the errors you see being made, and try to imagine how you would react if you were cycling amidst such behaviour – as surely you will be soon.

Try to stand in such a way that you can see the faces of drivers who should yield right of way. Where do they look, and for how long? What distracts their attention? Are they all confident in their actions, or are some experiencing problems? The answers to these kinds of questions should help you to appreciate the reality of modern traffic conditions, the degree of competence of drivers, and the difficulties that even the least vulnerable of road users endure. This knowledge should help you to cycle in a way which minimises difficulties for others, so that you, in turn, may have the maximum potential for a safe passage.

Look at traffic approaching the junction. Where is it maintaining speed, and where does it slow or accelerate? Where would be the best place to move to the centre of the road for a right turn, and what would be the likely effect on following vehicles? Try to get a feel for the capabilities of motor vehicles. Note how far it takes a car, a bus and a lorry to stop, both when driven well and driven badly. Estimate in advance how long it will take different vehicles to stop – and then see if you were right! The average length of a car (about 5 metres/16 feet) or the length of the road centre-line markings (usually 4 metres/13 feet at junctions) can help to judge these distances in a way that you can easily recall.

Note the sounds produced by different rates of acceleration and braking, as these can give you a good idea of your vulnerability from traffic when you are cycling. Note, too, how much room different vehicles need in traffic lanes of various widths, and judge whether you could safely share the same lane.

Having obtained a good assessment of general traffic conditions, look at the way the cyclists you see ride. What are their skills and faults and, in particular, do some of their actions put them into unnecessary danger? Which cyclists make the best progress through the junction and seem the most confident? How does the treatment given by others vary from one cyclist to another?

If you analyse these situations carefully, your confidence in traffic should be given a boost. It can be worth repeating this exercise at different locations.

4 — Riding along

Starting off

The first thing to decide about starting off is where to do so. In choosing a suitable place, you should consider your own safety, that of others whom you might impede, and whether or not, from a purely practical point of view, it is a good place.

Bad places are too near to a junction, on a tight bend or near the crest of a hill, between or immediately after parked vehicles or on steep uphill gradients. Good places are on straight roads where you are clearly visible from behind, and along a side road or drive from which you can turn left. It is worth wheeling your bike a short distance to a better location if there is one.

With your bike close to the kerb or road edge, mount from the kerbside and sit comfortably on the saddle. You should not start unseated, as this could cause you to swerve more than is necessary while gaining your balance. Place your right foot on its pedal, which should be moved to slightly forward of its uppermost position, and grasp both the handlebars and brakes. Applying the brakes now will prevent you moving while checking traffic and will also provide a quick, automatic check every time you start to ride that your brakes are in working order.

Always start in a gear about two below your normal riding gear so that you can get away quickly. With derailleur gears you should have anticipated this the last time you stopped and changed down. If you didn't do this, you will either have to change down now by lifting and rotating the rear wheel, or you must be prepared for a slow start for which you will require a longer gap in traffic.

Look over your shoulder for vehicles behind. As a suitable gap appears – you should aim not to interrupt the flow if possible – glance forward in case a pedestrian has suddenly stepped out in front of you or a car is pulling out or turning across your path. If clear, check backwards again, and then, looking ahead, start to move off. As soon as you have achieved good balance, you should glance behind once again so that you are absolutely sure what, if anything, is following, particularly if there are parked vehicles ahead to pass. This multiple checking forward and back should become a habit every time you start off, so that you cannot be caught unawares if something or someone suddenly appears from an unseen nook, however unlikely it might seem.

Generally, there is no need to signal when you start off, unless you have to steer to the right straight away in order to enter a moving traffic lane, but the golden rule with all signalling is to do so if it might help yourself, other traffic or pedestrians without itself putting you at risk.

If there is a continuous stream of traffic, one advantage of a cycle is that you can often move off when a wider vehicle would have to wait. This applies when the road is sufficiently wide that in moving off you will not interfere with moving traffic, and there are no parked vehicles immediately ahead.

Stopping

There are two normal types of stopping: stopping when you want to, and stopping when you have to. There is also emergency stopping, but this was covered in Chapter 2.

When it's your choice, always stop in similar places to those from which you can safely start. Keep clear of road junctions, tight bends and other places where you might impede traffic. Stopping at a junction is a common error by cyclists, especially when riding in groups, and one which is most frustrating to other road users, as well as being dangerous to everyone concerned. If you must stop near a junction to read a sign or map, always do so a few metres back, where you will not affect visibility, and always stop at the road edge, never in the middle.

One difference in the law as it applies to cyclists and motorists is that bicycles (without sidecars!) may stop where there are double white lines on the road. Treat this privilege sensibly; it is still unwise to stop on a bend or where other vehicles might be obliged to cross the centre lines.

Before stopping, be sure to change down to a gear about two below your normal riding gear, as this will make restarting easier. If an uphill restart is likely, change down still further. You can do this even if riding downhill, by pedalling against the brakes as you move the gear lever.

If there is other traffic about, or indeed if there are pedestrians, give the slowing down signal as you begin to stop. Descents apart, you should usually aim to stop without using your brakes, except for their final support as you set a foot down. This will give a smooth and gentle stop, save unnecessary brake wear and can even reduce hand fatigue by a noticeable amount on long journeys. Brakeless stopping requires the ability to judge just how far you will freewheel once you stop pedalling, and you should practise this. It is also useful to practise setting down either foot first when you stop.

Involuntary stops occur frequently in traffic – at junctions, restrictions and in traffic queues. You need to be able to use your brakes quickly. Try to anticipate the likelihood of stopping as much as possible by looking ahead, so that you can change down in gear. Rapid restarting is important in traffic, so if frequent stopping is likely, stay in a low gear.

It is also important that you should normally stop in the centre of the left-hand traffic lane and not towards its left side (Figure 4.1). This puts you in the position where you are most likely to be seen by other drivers and where they will be the least likely to pass you dangerously when restarting. Note, however, that whilst the centre-of-the-lane position will make you clearly visible in the inside rear view mirrors of most cars, you may well be in the blind area of vans, lorries, coaches and buses. The answer is not to move left or right, where you might encourage following drivers to squeeze past, but to allow extra room in front.

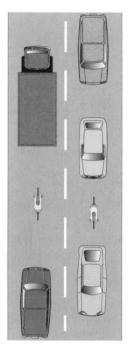

Figures 4.1
Stopping in traffic
Stop in the centre of the lane, at least 2 metres (nearly 7 feet) from the preceding vehicle, allowing extra distance behind large vehicles.

You should never stop closer than 2 metres (nearly 7 feet) behind a preceding vehicle; with larger vehicles, increase this distance. If there is any hint of a vehicle reversing, you will then have sufficient room to move out of the way.

In moving to the centre of a lane, it is important to signal your intentions to drivers behind, using a brief moving-right signal. Make sure that there is sufficient room for the manoeuvre.

Whenever you stop in traffic, get ready to restart straight away. With one foot on the ground and – at least for short stops – remaining seated on the saddle, get the other foot and pedal in the up position as quickly as you can. Toe clips make the changing of pedal positions very much easier.

On the move

Riding along, particularly in towns, entails a lot more than turning the pedals and manoeuvring at junctions. Not only must cyclists control their own vehicle, they must also continually compensate for the actions of others. Whereas a motorist whose concentration wanders may suffer nothing more than a dented car, a cyclist is much more at risk of personal injury and needs to be the most vigilant driver on the road. Whilst you should not hesitate to take your priority of passage when this applies, you should always act on the assumption that others will not respect it. Keeping relaxed but alert will enable you to deal best with difficult situations as they occur.

Observation and positioning (discussed below), are the two most essential skills to develop in traffic. After these comes conservation of momentum: when a cyclist provides all of the motive power from personal effort, it is a pity to waste it needlessly. Basically, the principle is to keep your momentum going by being sufficiently aware of conditions ahead that you can compensate for them by changing speed, rather than by stopping and restarting. Usually, this will mean slowing down, although sometimes a burst of acceleration can serve the purpose instead. Because a cyclist does not usually impede the passage of other vehicles, it is possible to determine your own pace more easily than other drivers, who are often subject to pressure to keep up with the traffic flow.

The principle of maintaining momentum leads to two related considerations:

- You should use your brakes as little as possible. Not only does their use waste valuable pedalling effort, but the performance of cycle brakes is not very good compared with those of other vehicles. It is better to use your brakes only when essential.

- When you slow down to approach a hazard, you should either cease pedalling completely or change to a lower gear. It will usually be less tiring, particularly on longer journeys, to use a lower gear than to alter your cadence, and there is the added advantage that you will be better prepared for stopping and restarting should it prove necessary.

Observation

Thinking ahead and planning every move is the hallmark of a skilled cyclist. For this, good observation is essential. If you cannot see and read exactly what is going on – in front, to your sides and behind – it will be impossible for you to plan the safest (and fastest) manoeuvre in any given situation. It is not enough to see every detail; you must also assess it and form a riding plan accordingly. For a cyclist, observation is not only about seeing, it is also about hearing. Many vital clues to the traffic situation are most easily assimilated by the ears.

The purpose of observation is to give you time to react to any hazard, whether it be actual or potential danger. Because of this need for reaction time, the degree of concentration necessary is proportional to both the complexity of the traffic situation and surroundings and the speed of traffic. Although you should always adjust your speed so that you can adequately observe the conditions around you, as a cyclist the level of concentration necessary will usually depend more on the speed of the other vehicles than on that of your own. You should realise, however, that as your speed increases you will need to concentrate further ahead and the foreground will become less distinct. Also, you will need a greater stopping distance for a given speed than a

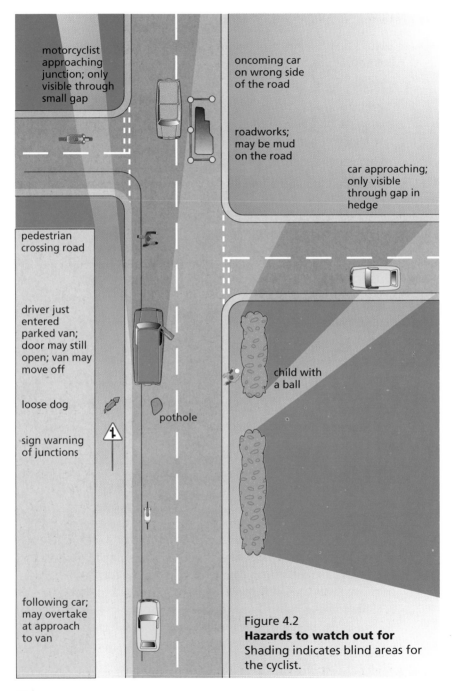

Figure 4.2
Hazards to watch out for
Shading indicates blind areas for the cyclist.

motor vehicle.

Local knowledge can help considerably in anticipating problems, but equally, familiarity can easily lead to a sense of false security. Always be guided by the prevailing conditions.

While riding along, look ahead as far as possible, but try to concentrate your surveillance on an area up to two or three vehicles ahead and spanning the full road width (Figure 4.2). Observe the obvious: vehicles turning into and from your road; the approach of junctions; parked vehicles and traffic queues. Note other drivers' signals, but never rely on them! Always wait for supporting evidence such as a reduction in speed or a change in direction.

Of equal importance, you should observe the small details which give such valuable clues to the less obvious:

- the presence of people in parked cars – they might open a door;

- exhaust fumes coming from a stationary vehicle – it might be about to move off;

- passengers moving on a bus – it might be about to stop;

- the last passenger entering or leaving a bus – it might be about to restart.

Near junctions, keep an eye on the wheels of vehicles in front – many drivers do not signal turns. Likewise, drivers in side roads and at roundabouts often take advantage of the approach of a cyclist to enter the traffic stream, with little appreciation of the speed of the cyclist or of the danger that they cause. Again, check for wheel movements. Sometimes a stern glance in their direction is all that is necessary to make an encroaching driver respect your right of way, but this is an acquired art, to be used only if you still have the ability to get yourself out of trouble.

Near shops, be wary of delivery vans – the driver may be concentrating more on unloading than on you. Likewise, the attention of the driver of a crowded car might be distracted, whilst unrestrained dogs in vehicles are often a menace to the driver's concentration. Shadows on the road, reflections in shop windows and vehicle lights at night can all give important clues of potential hazards. Don't keep your eyes *only* on the road ahead!

From time to time – and at the approach of any junction on your side of the road – it is important to glance over your shoulder so that you know what's happening behind you. Note what type of vehicles are following (cars, vans or lorries), how far behind the first one is, its width and approximately how fast it is going, and whether or not it is alone or the first in a stream.

Before looking behind, at this or any other time, always ensure that it is safe to do so. Check that you are not so close to a vehicle in front that you would hit it if it stopped suddenly, and that no one is about to cross your path. When looking behind, it is also important that your actions are not misinterpreted by others. It is amazing just how many drivers seem to think that because a cyclist has looked behind and seen them, they may immediately overtake. All too often the opposite is true, for the cyclist has looked behind as there is a hazard ahead. There are two possible responses to this:

- If conditions permit a longer look back, look the driver full in the face. This will often cause the driver to be more careful.

- Otherwise, it is useful to acquire the knack of looking behind discreetly, so that you can obtain the information you need without making it obvious that you have seen a following driver. To do this, move your eyes to the extreme but your head as little as possible.

Rearward observation needs to be complemented by listening. Learn to differentiate between normal sounds and those that mean danger. A common hazard at junctions is for a driver to overtake a cyclist and then to turn left sharply across the cyclist's path; another frequent problem occurs when a driver decides to overtake and then pulls in to stop. By detecting the change in pitch of a car's engine as the driver uses the accelerator, brakes, or changes gear, you will gain an important warning that these manoeuvres might occur, at a time when it is still safe to take compensatory action.

Look, too, at oncoming traffic. Is it going to turn across your path or encroach upon your space by overtaking? Again, wheel movements are more reliable indicators of actions than signals. Take particular care of the driver who has just given way to a car immediately ahead of you – that driver may restart without noticing you.

Look at the pedestrians you approach, particularly children, who may suddenly rush across the road. Are dogs on a lead and under control, or are they boisterous and likely to act unpredictably? Other cyclists, especially children, can also create a hazard.

The actions of other people are not the only hazards to observe. Roads themselves present problems. The position of trees, hedges and other side features can enable you to judge more easily the severity of bends and gradients. If the most distant point that you can see along a verge on either side of the road remains fixed, an approaching bend or hill is severe. If the point changes as you progress along the road, the bend or hill is more gradual. Take advantage of every opportunity to observe your surroundings. Breaks in hedges, for example, can sometimes give you a better view down a side road some way before a junction than it may be possible to obtain closer to it. The movement and lights of other vehicles might also help.

Traffic signs are significant aids to observation, and it is important that you understand the meaning of signs and markings. Even those signs which are not directly applicable to cyclists may give useful information about the way motorists might behave, and at night, on unlit roads, signs are particularly useful as warnings of what is coming. Although a cyclist will generally have more time to react to a sign than a motorist, you should nevertheless quickly observe and understand it, and then look beyond for the source of danger. It is the message that is important, not the sign!

Cyclists and the riders of other two-wheeled vehicles need to be particularly careful in scrutinising the condition of the road surface ahead. The presence of pot-holes and other surface irregularities is an obvious danger, and you will need advance warning in order to avoid them. But learn, too, to identify the different surface coverings which can give trouble: examples include snow, ice, oil, mud, loose stones, gravel and wet leaves. Oil and diesel fuel are often present on the road at the approach to other hazards; they are visible on dry roads, but often not when wet, although diesel's distinctive smell can be a useful clue. Likewise, ice can be very difficult to recognise in advance, and extra care needs to be taken when its presence is at all possible. Some surface types are themselves a hazard. Wooden blocks, stone setts, metal studs and many types of blockwork require great care. Concrete can hold surface water, and all these surfaces can trap ice long after it has disappeared elsewhere – and in a way which cannot be seen easily.

Take note, too, of the weather. Wind not only affects cyclists but also high-sided vehicles and caravans. It is best to keep clear of these. Spray thrown up by passing cars can affect your braking performance, even if it is not raining.

Having identified any hazard, the decision as to what you should do about it depends upon what can be seen, what can't, and the circumstances that might reasonably be expected to develop. It is important not to react just to what you have seen, and not to rush into any situation just because the driver in front does. It will also frequently be the case that there is more than one hazard at any one time, which may be related or quite independent of one another. You must prioritise the hazards on the basis of their significance, in order to direct your attention to best advantage.

The responses to many hazards will be found elsewhere in this book, but there will always be some situations where reactions cannot be learnt in advance. You should realise that, as you learn, mistakes may be made. It is therefore essential that all your decisions have a sufficient margin for error.

Positioning

We have already established that positioning is one of the most important traffic skills for a cyclist to acquire, yet it is precisely here that most cyclists perform badly. Many cyclists fail to position themselves properly because of their fear of traffic, yet ironically, it is this very fear that probably puts them most at risk.

There are two basic objectives of proper road positioning:

- to increase your margin of safety in relation to actual and potential danger by riding where you can obtain the best view, where you can best be seen by others and your movements predicted, and where you may deter movements by others which could be dangerous to yourself;

- to allow you to ride as direct a route as possible, conserving your energy and making control of the bicycle as simple as possible.

Good road positioning is *not* about keeping you out of the path of other traffic as much as possible. Contrary to popular belief, this is not necessarily the best way to maximise your safety.

Many cyclists, and probably the majority of the public at large, dread riding in close proximity to other traffic, because of the fear of being hit from behind. In fact, this type of collision is one of the least likely, accounting for no more than 5% of cycle–car casualties – and many of these are as a result of the cyclist swerving carelessly into traffic. Whilst no method of cycling is completely safe, you should not have to worry too much about rear hits if you cycle competently.

On the other hand, riding where traffic can see you clearly is likely to reduce your chances of having one of the much more common types of collision, which occur during turning or crossing manoeuvres. More collisions happen because drivers cannot see a cyclist or cannot anticipate the actions of the cyclist than because they do see but fail to take notice.

An important rule of road sharing is that no one should unnecessarily impede the passage of anyone else. However, you are quite justified in restricting the movements of other vehicles where this is important in protecting yourself, and you should not hesitate to do so when necessary.

Motorists primarily give their attention to that part of the highway where there is risk to themselves: they are not nearly so good at noticing anything outside their path. This zone of maximum surveillance is often very narrow, especially at higher speeds – it does not extend to much more than the moving traffic lane that the driver is following, plus the moving traffic lanes that are most likely to conflict with the driver's own movement. For you to be safest as a cyclist, you should ride within this zone of maximum surveillance, not outside it.

To understand positioning, you have to understand the concept of a moving traffic lane – that part of the carriageway along which through traffic normally moves. It is away from the area occupied by parked vehicles and other obstructions, and does not necessarily coincide with any markings on the surface. On a free-flowing road where markings are present, the moving traffic lanes are typically centred on the marked lanes, but do not embrace their full width.

Away from junctions, you should ride in one of two standard positions (see Figure 4.3), according to circumstances. The **primary riding position** is in the centre of the leftmost moving traffic lane for the direction in which you wish to travel. Here you will be well within the zone of maximum surveillance of both following drivers and those who might cross your path, and you will have the best two-way visibility of side roads and other features along the road. The road surface will usually be flatter here than it is nearer the edge, with fewer pot-holes and other problems, and this will afford easier control of your cycle. You should be able to maintain the straightest and fastest course without the need to deviate at side roads.

The primary riding position should therefore be your normal riding position when you can keep up with traffic, when you need to emphasise your presence to traffic ahead, or when you need to prevent following drivers from passing you dangerously. It is often the best position, too, on roads where there is no following traffic and on multi-lane roads where the traffic flow is light.

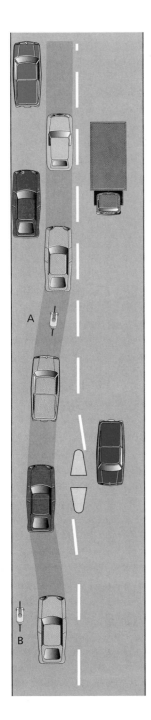

Because the primary riding position can result in some inconvenience to following drivers, it is reasonable to ride further to the left when this could help others, *as long as your own safety is not thereby impaired*. At these times you should adopt the **secondary riding position**, which is about 1 metre (3 feet) to the left of the moving traffic lane if the road is wide, but not closer than 0.5 metres (1.5 feet) to the edge of any road. Riding closer to the edge would leave you with no room for manoeuvre in the event of an emergency, whilst increasing the need to make unpredictable movements which could lead to a crash. You might also have to endure the discomfort and possible danger of drain covers, edge damage and the debris which tends to collect at the side of the road – and there is no reason why you should have a less comfortable journey than others. Riding too close to the edge can also make you difficult to see for drivers coming out of side roads and drives.

Only on long stretches of road where there are no side roads, drives or other entrances and you are travelling very slowly (perhaps up a hill) should you allow yourself to ride further to the left than the secondary riding position, but always keep at least 0.5 metres (1.5 feet) from the edge. Conversely, if you are travelling fast, keep further out.

On lightly-trafficked roads where you use the primary riding position, keep aware of

Figure 4.3
Standard riding positions
The moving traffic lane meanders to pass the traffic island and parked vehicles. Cyclist A is adopting the primary riding position, cyclist B the secondary riding position.

conditions behind you, with both eyes and ears. Always check behind when you see oncoming traffic, a bend or other hazard ahead. As soon as you sense a following vehicle, plan your move to the secondary position, so long as it is safe to do so. You should make your move neither too early nor too late, but gradually, in a way that causes no inconvenience to the other driver or to yourself. Because the move is done gradually and the position change is usually small, signalling is unnecessary.

On busy roads, it will be necessary to keep to the secondary riding position most of the time. There is no point in oscillating back and forth, as this will be more tiring for you and will probably confuse others. However, there are many occasions, even on busy roads, when you should use the primary position in order to benefit from the increased margin of safety that it provides.

When approaching every minor road and driveway which joins your side of a priority road, look as far as possible into that road to check for vehicles at or approaching the junction. You should start looking into the road from as far back as possible – in fact, as soon as you notice it. Look behind, too, to see if a following vehicle might be turning left. If you are absolutely sure that there is no hazard, you can maintain the secondary riding position. But if you are either unsure – perhaps because visibility is not too good – or if there is any vehicle which could cut across your path as you approach, move to the primary riding position until the junction is passed (Figure 4.4).

Never assume that, just because a vehicle has stopped, it will remain stationary, and in particular, don't trust drivers who approach a junction fast and then brake fiercely – move out! The primary riding position will:

• maximise the chances of you being seen and of your speed being appreciated;

• improve your own visibility of conditions ahead;

• provide an enhanced zone of safety should a driver cut across your path;

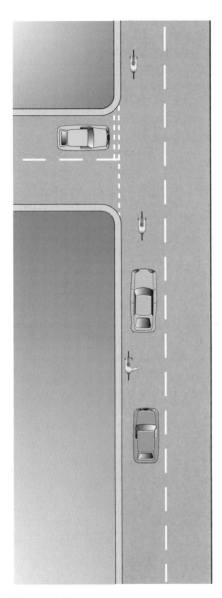

Figure 4.4
Changing position when passing a side road
If there is any danger, move to the primary riding positions to pass side roads. Keep clear of give way lines.

- help to dissuade any following driver from overtaking and then turning left.

It is, of course, necessary to make the movement from secondary to primary position with care. Don't leave it until you are too close to the junction – start to prepare the move as soon as you see any hazard, or suspect that conditions might make a decision difficult. Check behind for a suitable gap in traffic, signal right briefly if anyone is close, and then change position. So long as your secondary position was correct, the relatively small movement to the right that is necessary should not be difficult. Indeed, in many circumstances, if you start to move early, the deviation will be so slight that neither a gap in traffic nor signalling will be needed.

Also change to the primary riding position when the road surface near the edge is bad, perhaps because of a badly reinstated trench. Motorists are often less aware of surface conditions, and may not appreciate the real danger or discomfort these can cause for cyclists, so this change of position will need to be signalled well and made carefully. Where a really bad surface extends well into the road, keep further out still, but try not to allow sufficient room on your left for anyone to pass.

You should use the primary riding position when travelling on narrow or winding roads and at other types of narrowing (such as in traffic calming schemes) where overtaking could be dangerous. Where such conditions persist, however, as on some country lanes, do try to let traffic pass as soon as a suitable opportunity occurs, even if this requires you to slow down a little. You can never tell whether a driver behind is becoming impatient and might take a chance when it is least safe for you.

On tight left-hand bends, moving to the primary riding position will not only discourage dangerous overtaking, but can also improve both your forward visibility and your chances of being seen by drivers from both behind and ahead (Figure 4.5). Conversely, on right-hand bends the secondary position will usually improve visibility if there is little danger of you being passed. A further advantage of changing position at bends is that this can help to reduce the severity of the bend.

Further situations where a particular position should be adopted will be described in subsequent sections of this book. There is, however, one important general exception to the rules for

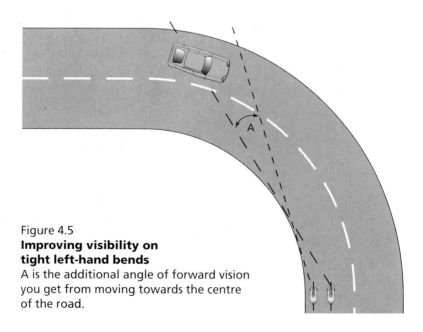

Figure 4.5
**Improving visibility on
tight left-hand bends**
A is the additional angle of forward vision
you get from moving towards the centre
of the road.

holding the primary riding position – when there is a significantly increased risk of being hit from behind. Bad visibility conditions such as fog, heavy mist or fine, persistent rain significantly increase the risk. Late evening, when the pubs close, is another time to be wary of: drivers who have been drinking cannot be relied upon to control their vehicles with an acceptable degree of skill. At each of these times, it is prudent to keep further left and to take extra care near junctions.

You may also find it difficult to move to the primary riding position along narrow main roads where traffic is fast and continuous. Your only option here is to ride as best you can and reduce speed at hazards if you cannot move out. At all times, take particular care to hold a straight course by grasping the handlebars firmly.

One final consideration about positioning concerns riding with another cyclist. Except where a road is both narrow *and* busy (a matter for judgement), cyclists may ride two, but never more, abreast. This is the most sociable way to ride as you are able to converse more readily with one another, and it also enables you to be seen even more easily by traffic. Unfortunately, some motorists do not appreciate that the law permits cyclists to ride in this way – they seem to forget that two cyclists side by side take up less road space than a lone car driver – and from time to time you may meet some who, from their gestures, clearly feel that you are acting wrongly.

Of course, if you do seem to be causing a real problem to people behind, with regard to the traffic flow, it is sensible to move back to single file. It is particularly helpful to do this for lorries and buses, which need more room to pass. To move to single file, the cyclist nearest the centre of the road should initiate the action by accelerating or easing off (braking should not normally be necessary), while the second rider co-operates by doing the opposite. It is usually easiest if the cyclist nearest the centre moves in behind the other.

Forward clearance

In normal moving traffic a cyclist does not have to worry too much about keeping clear of vehicles in front, but in towns and other places where traffic speeds are low it becomes a necessary consideration. Getting too close to the back of another vehicle has two dangers. You may be less visible to the driver (for example, you may not be reflected in wing mirrors), and you will be very vulnerable if the driver suddenly slams on the brakes (Figure 4.6). In addition, the closer you are to the vehicle in front, the less you will see beyond it.

A good clearance to maintain is about 2 metres (nearly 7 feet) for every 5 km/h or so (3 mph), with an absolute minimum of 3 metres (10 feet). Holding the primary riding position should deter overtaking into this space by anyone behind.

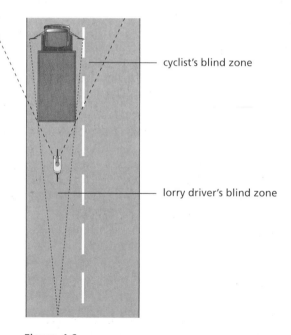

cyclist's blind zone

lorry driver's blind zone

Figure 4.6
Forward clearance
Riding too close to a vehicle in front reduces your visibility, and others' visibility of you.

5 —— Everyday manoeuvres

The movements described in this chapter are the basic building blocks of cycling that need to be learnt by all cyclists. Learn them well, and ensure that you do not establish bad habits.

Signalling

By definition, all movements involve a change in your position on the road, and often a change relative to the position of following vehicles in a way that might not easily be predicted. Clear signalling of movements is therefore important in order to inform others and to enhance your own safety. You must realise, though, that a signal is merely a warning of intention, not an instruction. It conveys no right of way, and you should be quite sure that a movement is safe to make, without unduly inconveniencing others, before executing it. The hand signals you should use when cycling were illustrated in fig 2.4. You will find additional notes concerning the use of signals by cyclists in other sections of this book.

The general principle, however, is to signal when, and for as long as, a signal can convey useful information to another road user (including pedestrians). You should therefore signal before making an unpredictable movement, maintaining it as long as possible while you are making the move, but there's little point in keeping your arm stretched out while in the middle of a stationary queue of traffic. You should also return both hands to the handlebars immediately before making a turn in order to be in complete control of your cycle in the event of any unevenness of the surface.

Overtaking

Overtaking is a manoeuvre you will have to use often, and one for which correct positioning is important. In most cases, cyclists only overtake stationary vehicles and other kerbside obstructions, but even here dangers are still present, such as a door opening into your path or a vehicle moving off as you pass. To change traffic lanes in order to pass obstructions requires confidence and the use of the proper technique.

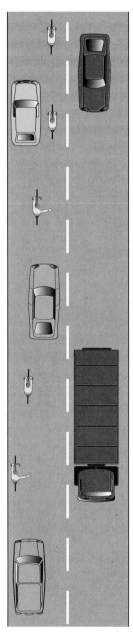

You should start to prepare for overtaking an obstruction as soon as you first see it. From this time onwards be sure to keep track of the progress of vehicles following you, so that you are fully conversant with what is happening behind. Well in advance – as much as 100 metres (about 330 feet) on free-flowing roads – take the first opportunity to move to the right of the traffic lane (marked or imaginary) that is obstructed (Figure 5.1). This should not be too difficult, as other traffic will also be moving out for the same reason. If you are passing a car, look through the rear window as you approach to see if there is anyone inside. Look, too, for exhaust fumes or any other tell-tale signs of imminent movement of the vehicle or occupants.

About 20 metres (60 feet or so) back from the obstruction – more on fast roads – glance behind to check that no one is too close, then signal right and move out to overtake. You should pass any vehicle with at least 1.5 metres (5 feet) to spare, just in case a door is thrown open. If this would leave space to your right where you could be overtaken, but not safely, you should move out further to block this. Generally, the primary riding position should be used for overtaking, but allow at least 2 metres (nearly 7 feet) clearance when passing a lorry or bus.

If you do not have to cross a marked traffic lane in order to overtake, you will have right of way over the vehicles following you, although you should take care that this is respected. On the other hand, if it is necessary to cross a lane marking, you must give way to traffic already in the second lane before entering it. This may require you to slow down a little until a suitable gap arrives (keep looking behind), or even to stop.

Figure 5.1
Overtaking

For busy roads, Chapter 6 will describe how to negotiate your way into the traffic stream.

If there are a number of stationary vehicles to pass, maintain a straight line past all of them, keeping at least 1.5 metres (5 feet) from any. Never weave back and forth, and do not move left if there is a short gap in parking. Drivers may take advantage of any apparent opportunity for them to pass, and you could have difficulty moving back. You will also be moving out of their principal area of surveillance and putting yourself more at risk; remember that parked cars can easily mask a cyclist who is out of the moving traffic lane. Don't worry if keeping to the lane seems to impede following traffic – it is not safe for it to pass anyway.

If there is a longer gap in parking – about 30 metres (100 feet or so) or more – move to the secondary riding position (just left of the moving traffic lane) if this would allow others to pass you safely, but make sure that you can move out again easily well before reaching the next parked vehicle. Of course, where the moving traffic lane goes left, you should follow it.

When overtaking, look out especially for pedestrians, children, cats and dogs who might move out between parked vehicles. They are another reason for not getting too close. High-sided vehicles pose a particular problem in this respect, as you will not be able to see over them. When passing such a vehicle, move further out than usual, slacken speed and have your hands ready on the brakes. Take similar precautions near obvious attractors of children, such as ice-cream vans and school buses.

If a driver starts to pull out in front of you, slow down to let the driver go if possible, but if it is too late to do this, accelerate to get past, steering to the right. However, if a driver is only signalling an intention to pull out, it is usually best for a cyclist not to give way. Do, however, keep well clear, and keep an eye on the movement of the vehicle's front wheels.

Sometimes your side of the road will be largely or completely blocked. The most dangerous situation is when a cycle could pass a stationary vehicle without straddling the centre line, but a car couldn't. Under these circumstances the driver of the obstructing vehicle (a bus at a stop, for example) might not expect anyone to be able to pass and could take insufficient care when restarting. Long vehicles are more difficult to pass in any case. You shouldn't try to overtake within such a limited space unless you are quite sure that the vehicle will not suddenly move off and that there is enough 'escape room'. It is often better to wait.

If your side of the road is completely blocked, it will be necessary to cross the centre line in order to overtake. Be sure that there is nothing coming in the opposite direction before proceeding. Again, it is better not to overtake a long vehicle in this way if it has only stopped temporarily.

There are times when cyclists need to overtake moving vehicles – other cyclists, tractors, milk floats, even slow cars and lorries. Before doing so, be quite sure that overtaking is really necessary. There is little point overtaking a slow truck near the top of a hill if it will soon speed up and then overtake you!

Never overtake a moving vehicle on the left side within the same traffic lane. Also ensure that you have sufficient speed to overtake, and sufficient safe distance in which to do so. A cyclist's ability to accelerate out of danger is limited, and even a gentle hill can make all the difference. Always look ahead of the vehicle you intend to overtake for bends, obstructions and other dangers – overtaking will often take longer than you think. You should usually allow any following vehicle to overtake you first if possible – it is better to follow than to be pursued.

Once you have decided to overtake, adopt the normal overtaking procedure, ensuring that the driver of any vehicle to be overtaken can see your signal in the mirror. If that vehicle speeds up as you pass – it should ease off to let you by – slip back. Until you have passed half the length of the vehicle, you can change your mind if necessary and slip back quite easily. After that, you should normally continue, particularly if you are being followed by someone else. Of course, if some new danger appears, easing back may still be the best reaction.

If there was only a small difference in speed between yourself and the other vehicle, do not pull in too quickly after overtaking. The sideways movement will reduce your forward speed a little, and you could then be hit from behind.

Being overtaken

Because other drivers often do not appreciate the danger that they can present to a cyclist when overtaking, it is necessary to be alert to this problem. The use of positioning to deter overtaking when it is not safe has already been described, and by adopting the recommended riding positions you will leave yourself room for manoeuvre if someone passes too close. But there are other problems to bear in mind, too.

One of these is caused by the close passage of long vehicles. Although professional drivers are usually amongst the most skilled, sometimes they do not allow adequately for the speed of a cyclist. The front of a long vehicle may pass with plenty of clearance, but the tail end of a trailer can swing back to the left too soon and threaten a cyclist who has progressed further than was anticipated. This is a particular problem on narrow roads when overtaking takes place during relatively short gaps in oncoming traffic. To help the situation, it is wise for a cyclist to ease off pedalling when being overtaken by a long vehicle, and to be ready to brake if necessary in order to keep clear of the rear end. In extreme cases

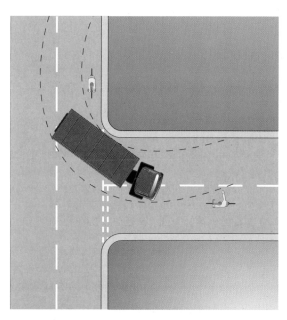

Figure 5.2
Turning path of a long vehicle at a road junction

you may even have to get off the road quickly, but this will be a very rare situation for a cyclist who has positioned properly.

Long vehicles also present problems on left-hand bends and when the driver wants to turn left at a junction (Figure 5.2). In both cases the middle of the vehicle moves further left than its ends, and the driver will need to steer well to the right to avoid colliding with an adjacent cyclist. Such collisions are often fatal. If you see a long vehicle coming up behind on the approach to such a left turn, you can encourage the driver either to give you more room or to wait until it is safer to overtake by moving further out yourself. **If you are behind a long vehicle at a junction or in a queue, never edge forward alongside it.** Take care, too, if you are leaving a road into which a long vehicle is turning in the opposite direction, for it may well swing over into your side of the road.

High-sided vehicles can also present problems, particularly when it is windy. As they pass you they can provide a break from the wind, but they are followed by eddy currents which can easily force a cyclist off course and cause a spill. The suction effect of large vehicles can be considerable and is one of the biggest dangers to a cyclist on the roads. To minimise the problems, pedal to increase your stability as you are passed, but do so against the brakes if necessary in order to keep your speed down. Hold the handlebars firmly, ready to resist any change of direction, and crouch low. Strong crosswinds can deflect a high vehicle across the road in a way that has to be seen to be believed, and this can also create a distinct danger for any other road user.

Caravans towed by cars can cause problems similar to long and high-sided vehicles, whilst their drivers – who are frequently much less experienced that lorry drivers – often only allow for a car's width when overtaking. Treat caravans with caution, and be alert for extension mirrors protruding from the side of the car.

The greatest overtaking danger to a cyclist comes not from traffic behind, but from ahead. When a cyclist is travelling alone on one side of a road, an unfortunate number of oncoming drivers use the opportunity to overtake vehicles ahead of them, encroaching upon the cyclist's path. Little thought seems to be given to the implications for the cyclist, who would almost certainly be killed in any head-on collision. If such an overtaking procedure starts when you are close, there is little you can do about it except to keep left and hold on firmly. However, the manoeuvre will often commence well ahead, perhaps because you haven't been seen. Here, with care, you can take deterrent action. After ensuring that there really is no one behind you, pull out further right, but be ready to go quickly left. It can take some nerve to steer towards an oncoming car and to hold this position for long, but the situation really is a desperate one. More often than not, the oncoming driver will soon realise that you are there and that there is an element of danger, and will move in. However, if the driver is intent on holding course, go left in good time and hold on tight.

Turning left

The left turn is the simplest manoeuvre for a cyclist to make, but even here there are consequences that need to be considered.

If visibility is good in all directions and you know that you will neither have to stop at the junction nor be followed by any other vehicle turning left, you can turn left maintaining a secondary riding position, if that is how you approached the junction. In all other circumstances, you should first adopt the primary riding position, however odd it may seem to move right in order to turn left (Figure 5.3). **It is a common mistake for cyclists to keep too far left at all turns.**

As you turn, look out for other vehicles which may cross your path from the right. Normally, you will have the right of way, but at some turns where there is a specific turning lane, road markings give priority to the right, and you must heed this. Look out for pedestrians crossing the road and give way to them if you can (but see Chapter 7). Then look into the road into which you are turning to check for parked cars and other obstructions on the left which you may need to pass. If there are any, start to move to the right straight away to give yourself room to pass them. You should not allow other traffic to pass you in the same traffic lane until you are sure that it is safe for it to do so.

Signalling a left turn might seem an elementary courtesy which is easy to do. Unfortunately, due to the behaviour of a significant minority of drivers, this is not always as desirable for a cyclist as it should be. Some drivers, who themselves wish to turn left, take any indication that a cyclist ahead of them is doing likewise as an invitation to overtake at the junction, cutting across the

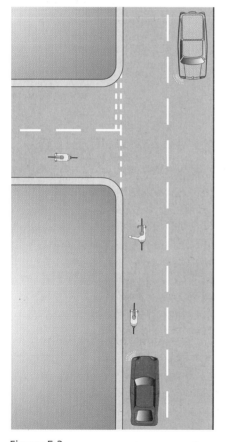 

Figure 5.3
Left turns
If there is any danger, and always where there is a turning lane, turn left from the primary riding position.

cyclist's path in a very dangerous manner. Even the primary riding position does not protect a cyclist completely against this behaviour. Obviously, you should judge the prevailing conditions for yourself and be courteous to others when possible, but the general advice is to signal left only immediately before you turn and when it is unlikely to cause any danger to yourself.

If there is a separate left-turn lane at a junction, use it, but always ride in the primary riding position to deter overtaking. If there is an island at the junction between a single turning lane and the rest of the carriageway, take particular care that you are not 'squeezed' at the point where the island starts. Again, the primary riding position will give you room for manoeuvre, whilst a brief moving-right signal at the approach to the island can often discourage a driver who seems likely to overtake and cut in front.

Going ahead at junctions

This section is about crossing more important junctions, where there is a significant amount of crossing or turning traffic. Passing minor side roads was described in Chapter 4. You should always adopt the primary riding position on the approach and maintain it until you are completely through the junction and it is safe for others to pass (see Figure 5.4). Although you should keep yourself aware of the complete traffic situation throughout the manoeuvre, your attention at the approach to an important junction should be particularly concerned with ensuring that others do not overtake and then cut in front of you to turn left.

A short moving-right signal can be useful for emphasising to following drivers that you are exercising your priority to go ahead, particularly where a left deceleration lane (i.e., one which is built out from the main carriageway) is provided. Although it is best not to confuse others if at all possible, giving a moving-right signal, even though you are not intending to go right, will at least encourage others to take more care than might otherwise be the case. As in all cases, you must ride to suit the circumstances and to ensure your own safety.

As you get closer to the junction, you should concern yourself first with traffic crossing or turning right across your path, and then with vehicles pulling out from the left. If at all possible, take the priority which is yours and, by changing your position

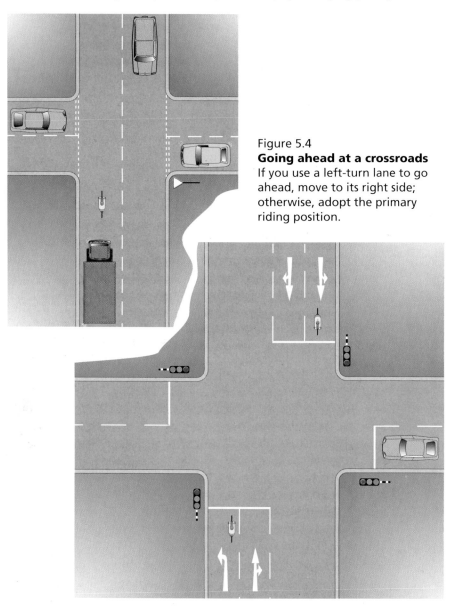

Figure 5.4
Going ahead at a crossroads
If you use a left-turn lane to go ahead, move to its right side; otherwise, adopt the primary riding position.

or signalling, or both, discourage others from usurping it. However, always ensure that you leave yourself a sufficient margin of safety to allow for the aggressive driver who flouts all the rules, and try to avoid making any movement too suddenly. Take extra care if you are masked from any drivers by turning traffic or congestion, and always keep your hands over the brakes.

An important general rule for junctions is to regard any give way or stop markings on a road which intersects with the one you are on as indicating a zone of danger. It is precisely at these places that most collisions between cycles and motor vehicles take place. **Always give a wide berth to give way and stop markings.**

If there is a left-turn lane which, because of its design, is unlikely to be used other than by traffic turning left, you should keep out of it and use the left-hand ahead lane. Maintaining the primary riding position should avoid any ambiguity as to where you are going. Indeed, it is always best to use the appropriately marked lane for going ahead if this is possible, but there are times when such action can result in unacceptable risks for a cyclist under real-life traffic conditions. The most common occasion is where there is a left-turn lane marked on the road, but with no physical separation from the ahead lane(s). The danger in using the theoretically correct lane in such circumstances is simply that many motorists don't, and you could easily find yourself overtaken on the left as you cross the junction. A cyclist is vulnerable to traffic passing on both sides at the same time, and it is very difficult to look rearwards in both directions at once. The answer, therefore, is to keep to the left-hand lane at these junctions, but to occupy a position to its right-hand side in order to suggest to following drivers that you might not be making the marked turn. You should take care, however, not to leave sufficient room to your left for anyone to pass.

If a turning lane is controlled by a separate filter traffic signal, you should not use it for ahead movements. And if there is more than one marked left-turn lane, use the right-hand of these to go ahead if necessary. Never use a lane further to the left. Often the

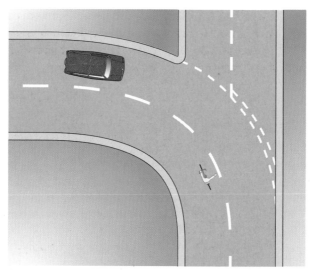

Figure 5.5
Going ahead off a major road

second or third lane will be marked for both left-turning and ahead movements and you should use the leftmost lane that is so marked. Whenever you do use a lane away from the left side of the road, always bear in mind the possibility that someone might pass on your left, and do not move back towards the left side until you are sure that this will not happen.

Another type of ahead movement which is difficult is where the road required lies straight ahead, but the road you are on turns left (Figure 5.5). Here you need to treat the manoeuvre as a right turn and to use the procedures described in the next section for making it. Take care, however, not to get too close to the centre line before being sure that there is no oncoming traffic, as this might be going fast and could cut the corner. It is better to stay back, even if this means temporarily blocking following vehicles.

The simpler right turn

The right turn is the most difficult turn for cyclists, as it is necessary to cross every lane of traffic. However, by following the correct technique, right turns can be carried out with no great risk on all but the fastest of roads. This section describes the technique when turning right off a through road.

One of the first requirements is to identify just where the right turn is. You will need to have this information much earlier than for a left turn. In the absence of good local knowledge, direction signs can be useful, but on faster roads these will usually occur too early for a cyclist to start manoeuvring. The movement of traffic ahead might provide more useful clues as to where the turning is. If you get too close to the turn before moving right, you will have to stop on the left and await a suitable gap in traffic before proceeding. **Never swerve suddenly or cross moving traffic at too great an angle or without making the proper preparations.**

If the road from which you are turning has only a single lane in each direction and traffic flows are light, turning right is quite easy. From about 100 metres (about 330 feet) before the junction, keep track of the movement of any following vehicles by looking behind at least twice. Look, too, at oncoming traffic in case it might be about to cross the centre line for any reason. At about 50 metres (about 140 feet), look behind again and select a suitable gap in traffic. Signal right clearly, and move smoothly but quickly towards the centre of the road (Figure 5.6a). Keep an eye on following vehicles as you cross, but transfer more of your attention towards the traffic coming towards you. As you approach the junction you should be about 1 metre (3 feet) from the centre line, but always be prepared to move left if other vehicles come too close.

If you are turning with other traffic, take up a position slightly left of the centre line of those vehicles, in order to deter overtaking. If there is a marked right-turn lane, use it and adopt the primary riding position. Where there is more than one right-turning lane, use the leftmost one.

If there is any traffic approaching which could conflict with your turn, wait at the junction opposite the centre line of the new road. Continue to signal while you wait. On lightly trafficked roads it is often possible to adjust your speed in order to avoid arriving at the junction at the same time as anyone else. When there is a sufficient gap in traffic, turn right as quickly as you can.

If the new road has only one lane in your direction of travel, your position on entering it should be between the centre of that lane and the middle of the road. Do not enter too far to the left or you may encourage a following driver to overtake you in the turn, or you may have to move out again to pass an obstruction. On the other hand, take care that no one can pass to your left, or that a driver leaving the new road does not come out into your path. Remember, too, to keep well clear of the hazard zone near the give way or stop lines.

If the new road has more than one lane in your direction, enter the left-hand lane between its centre and right side – do not cut across the other lanes. Whatever the road, take up the primary riding position after entering it until you are sure that there are no obstructions to pass and it is safe for others to overtake you.

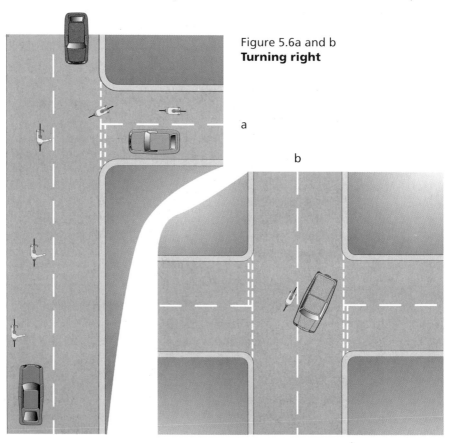

Figure 5.6a and b
Turning right

a

b

The technique described for entry to another road can be applied to all types of right turn. However, if the major road is busy, the approach will be more difficult and involves use of the more advanced technique of negotiation. This will be described in Chapter 6.

Sometimes at a crossroads you will be turning right at the same time as another vehicle from the opposite direction. The normal rule here is that you first pass each other right side to right side and then turn (Figure 5.6b). In some places, however, road markings indicate that such turns should be made left side to left side without passing. You should stick to the normal rule unless markings indicate to the contrary, but always be alert to the fact that others may act differently. In all cases, be very careful if a queue of vehicles waiting to turn masks visibility of oncoming traffic. Nose out inch by inch until you can see better.

A different type of right turn is where the marked priority road turns right but another, more minor road goes straight ahead (Figure 5.7). In one sense, this is not really a right turn at all as you will have priority over traffic on the secondary road. But don't count on it! In some places, traffic going ahead can be in the majority, and local drivers rushing to get home might not

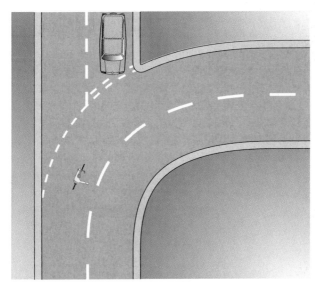

Figure 5.7
Turning right with a main road

expect a cyclist to be going right. It is wise to adopt the primary riding position approaching such a junction, and also to signal right, even though this is not strictly necessary. Watch out for traffic ahead and behind.

Leaving minor roads

The movements described so far have assumed that you start on a road which has priority, either continuing along the same road or turning onto one of lower priority. The reverse movements – from a minor road onto or across a major road – differ in that you will usually be less at risk before the junction, but more at risk while passing through it (Figure 5.8). Whichever way you are going, the object of positioning is the same – to stop anyone behind from overtaking you in a dangerous manner, and to give you the best view of the major road traffic.

If there is only one lane in your direction, occupy the primary riding position for any movement, unless the lane is very wide, in which case you should ride about 2 metres (nearly 7 feet) left

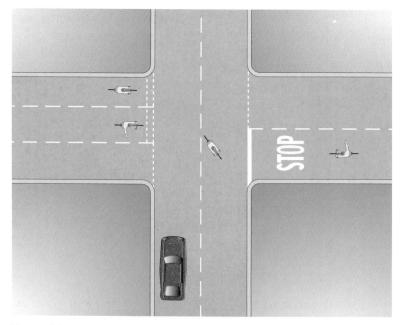

Figure 5.8
Leaving minor roads

of the centre line to turn right. Getting any closer to the centre line puts you at risk from traffic turning into your road. If there are two or more lanes, occupy the primary riding position in the appropriate lane.

Unless there are traffic signals, the junction will be controlled with either a give way or a stop sign directed at your road. If there is a give way sign, you do not need to stop if there is a clear passage, but you must be prepared to do so if necessary. Therefore, approach slowly, changing down in gear, to give yourself plenty of time to survey the traffic situation. Where possible, it is better not to stop, as you will waste valuable momentum; just as important, you will cross the major road more slowly after a restart and therefore be at risk for longer. However, unless you are quite sure that it is safe to proceed, you should stop. Where there is a stop sign, you have no choice. Such signs are usually placed where visibility is bad, at least from a motor vehicle. Sometimes the stop requirement is less appropriate for a cyclist, but you must always obey it.

From time to time you will find that a driver on the major road offers you the right of way, even though it is not strictly yours. Such an invitation may take the form of a wave for you to proceed, the flashing of headlights, or simply an obvious slowing down or stopping. This friendly gesture should, if possible, be accepted, but don't do so too readily. Although one driver may be willing for you to take precedence, another driver may not, or the latter may simply have not understood the intentions of the first. Whenever you are offered priority, first check in all directions that it really would be safe to accept. If so, say a polite 'thank you' by raising your right hand briefly as you proceed. However, if to accept would place you in any danger, refuse the offer by waving the driver past. Unfortunately, some offers of right of way, though well intended, can considerably complicate a manoeuvre and make you wish that you'd been left to your own means.

When the way is clear, proceed across or turn as desired, occupying the primary riding position on the second road, at least until it is safe to do otherwise. When turning right, don't

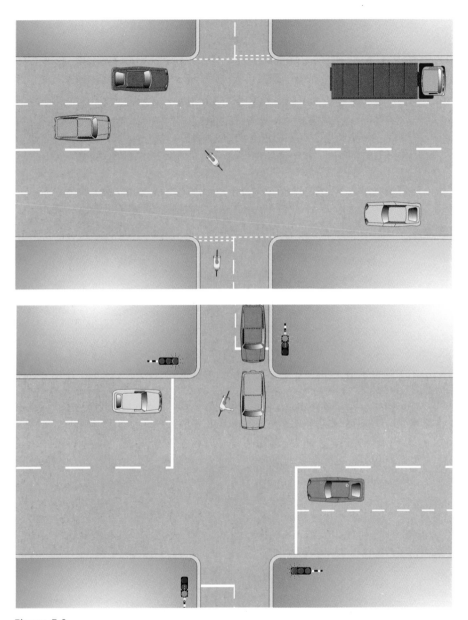

Figure 5.9
Crossing multi-lane roads
If you need to pause when crossing, face approaching traffic with your cycle at 45°
to the main road.
If you are held up by oncoming traffic when turning right, wait in the furthest lane.

cut corners; imagine an island at the point where the centre lines of the two roads would meet, and turn around this, keeping left. By doing this, you will ride the shortest distance across the major road and be at risk for the minimum time.

If going ahead or right at a crossroads, watch out for traffic from the opposite direction. Wherever it goes it affects, and has priority over, your right turn. If it intends to turn right, it should give way to you going ahead, but don't rely on this. Sometimes, drivers deliberately cut in front when turning right, either to minimise their own time at risk or because they misjudge the speed of a cyclist.

When crossing a dual carriageway, it will usually be possible for you to treat it as two separate roads, pausing in the middle if necessary. Because a cycle is shorter than a car, this may well be an easier movement for a cyclist than for a car driver. Sometimes, too, it will be necessary to wait in the middle of a multi-lane non-dual carriageway road. If you do this, you should wait with the cycle at about 45° to the main road – in this position you will take up less space yet be clearly visible. Obviously this will not be necessary if you can be protected by the cover of a car making the same movement. If you are held up while turning right by a queue of traffic from the opposite direction, wait in the furthest lane of the major road so that you will have the minimum distance to cross after restarting (Figure 5.9).

No-priority junctions

Most junctions of any importance have priority markings in one direction or another in order to regulate the flow of traffic and to increase safety. However, there remain many junctions with no indication of priority, particularly in residential districts and on country lanes.

At T-junctions, the acknowledged order of priority is that straight-through vehicles crossing the T go first, followed by those turning into and then out of the stem of the T. In effect, the priorities are the same as if there were give way markings to favour the through road.

At unmarked crossroads the situation is more complicated, and there is no clear priority at all. There is no universal priority-from-the-nearside rule in Britain as in Europe. Indeed, the only guideline is that crossing traffic from any direction invariably assumes precedence over traffic turning. The answer is to treat whichever road you are using as one where you should give way, and to proceed cautiously. In practice, though, traffic flows at these junctions are usually so light that problems do not often arise.

Traffic signals

Traffic signals are generally well-liked by cyclists, providing one of the safest ways for them to traverse busy junctions. However, it should not be thought that the presence of signals necessarily makes for a safe junction. A combination of the complexity of movements, the tendency of some drivers to proceed before or after the green light and the frequent presence of large numbers of pedestrians can easily lead to situations where collisions happen.

From a cyclist's point of view, the greatest hazard is not being seen by other drivers. With their concentration already attracted by the signals themselves, a cyclist can be overlooked, so it is necessary to make yourself as conspicuous as possible by positioning.

If you intend to go straight ahead or turn left, occupy the primary riding position at the approach to signals, whether they be at red or green. If you are turning right, occupy the centre of the right-hand lane. In either case, do not allow any other vehicle to share the same lane to the side of you. This will maximise your chances of being seen from both behind and ahead, and also protect you from close overtaking as the signals change. On multi-lane roads, the general lane-taking advice already given for junctions applies.

Approaching signals, change down in gear unless you think that you can keep going. If you're proved wrong and have to stop, brake hard if it is safe to do so, and change down quickly. Although Chapter 8 will discuss the special circumstances of overtaking in congested streets, it is usually foolish to creep up the inside of queues at signals, as you will not be easily seen by drivers. **Never pass a bus or long vehicle in the same lane near the head of a signal queue.** At some locations, advanced stop lines have been introduced for cyclists. These are discussed in Chapter 10.

The rules for obeying traffic signals apply to cyclists as much as to anyone else. If they're at red you must stop, and if they're at green you may pass, but only if it is safe to do so. Look out particularly for pedestrians making a last-minute dash across the road, or the driver who jumps the change to red in the other direction. You should also not pass unless the junction is sufficiently clear that you can go straight through, though this will seldom be a problem for a cyclist.

A single amber signal means that you should stop unless you are so close to the stop line that to pull up might cause a collision. As you are the likely casualty of any crash, you should be particularly careful about this one – don't pull up so sharply that a following vehicle could run into you. You should be able to tell from the sound of its engine whether or not a car behind is likely to stop; if not, keep going yourself.

The red-and-amber signal also means 'stop', being merely an indication that green is to follow. Traffic should not move at all on this signal, but it often does, and it is recommended that you use this phase to gain your balance. In this way you can get off to a quick start on the green, and you will be less likely to be overtaken dangerously in the junction. You can do this quite legally if you make a point of stopping just a metre (3 feet) back from the stop line, for that distance should be quite sufficient for you to push off and balance before the signals change to green. Do not do this, however, if this movement might antagonise any pedestrians who are still crossing.

Watch out for filter signals, and do not use a filter lane unless you are turning. In Britain, but not in most other countries, the illumination of a green left or right arrow indicates that vehicles turning in that direction are protected from oncoming traffic.

A final point on traffic signals concerns their actuation – the mechanism that makes them change to green in your favour. Often this is no problem for cyclists, there being plenty of other traffic about to do the job for you. But late at night or early in the morning, things may be different, and yours may be the only vehicle on the road. If you don't want a delayed journey, it will then be necessary to ensure that you change the signals yourself. Most modern signals are actuated by induction loops, buried under the road surface – their location is marked by box-like patterns in the tarmac. Be sure to pass over these (Figure 5.10). If there's no other traffic about, you can maximise your chance of being detected by riding diagonally across the box so that as much of your cycle as possible is within it.

Some signals simply won't respond to cycles. Most are capable of doing so, but their sensitivity is set incorrectly. If you find that you can't actuate a change to green in your favour and there's no other traffic on your road, you will have little choice but to proceed through the red light. Be extremely cautious about this, though – traffic on the other arms of the junction won't expect

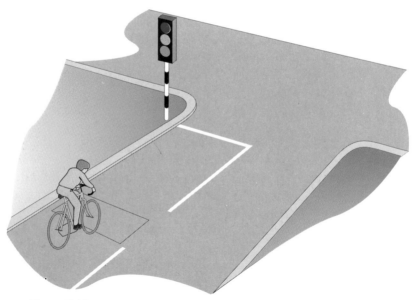

Figure 5.10
Actuating traffic signals

you to be moving. You may be able to proceed more easily if you walk.

Roundabouts

Roundabouts are now to be found on all kinds of roads, and most cyclists will need to encounter them from an early stage. Many roundabouts on local roads pose no great difficulty for cyclists, but others, which are not always easy to distinguish by design, are associated with increased risk and high casualty rates. For this reason, advice on roundabouts is grouped together in this book in Chapter 6. You should read through this and apply it to the roundabouts that you meet.

Roadworks and diversions

Minor roadworks are much the same as any other form of obstruction – you pass using the usual techniques for overtaking, taking particular care in case the road surface is uneven or muddy. Where works involve a long length of road, though, one or more lanes may be closed, all traffic being channelled into the remaining space. On two-lane roads a shuttle lane is often created, traffic using the lane first in one direction and then the other (Figure 5.11). Control may be by traffic signals or by

Figure 5.11
Shuttle lanes
Take the centre of a narrow lane, in order to deter overtaking. If only one or two vehicles are behind you, let them go first.

manual 'Stop–Go' boards. These situations can be hazardous for a cyclist if following vehicles try to squeeze past in too narrow a space, or if oncoming traffic proceeds before you are clear. The rule is to ride as you would on a road of corresponding width; occupy the primary riding position unless it is safe for you to be passed, having full regard to the condition of the surface. Try not to worry about delaying other traffic, but on the other hand, do pass along the lane as quickly as you can.

More substantial works sometimes require the closure of a road in one or both directions, and the diversionary route can add significant extra distance, perhaps via busier roads. In most cases, cyclists are still able to pass a closure, if only by dismounting, but it can be a gamble to ignore a diversion sign if you do not know what's ahead. If possible, ask someone living locally. In the country, look carefully at a map for the likely location of a closure. If there is a bridge which might have fallen or a new road under construction, your path is more likely to be barred. Otherwise, you will probably be able to proceed. You should not ride against the flow on a road signed for one-way working.

Taking the wrong route

Everyone makes mistakes, so inevitably there will be times when you make the wrong manoeuvre, such as turning into the wrong road or using an incorrect direction lane at a junction. This may be because you are a stranger in the locality or because traffic conditions make it difficult to follow the correct route.

In either case, you should normally follow through your mistake and only then make a correction. Only if you are absolutely sure that there could be no inconvenience or danger to yourself or anyone else should you change lanes at a junction, turn from the wrong lane or change direction in an unexpected manner.

The simplest form of correction is often to proceed through a junction, then stop and, when clear, make a U-turn. In one-way streets, a series of left or right turns may solve your problem, or it might be easier to dismount and walk to the correct road.

6 —— The more difficult manoeuvres

There was a time, little more than a generation ago, when the ordinary right turn was considered to be the most difficult manoeuvre that a cyclist had to make. Since then, the preoccupation of traffic planners with accommodating growth in motor traffic, and the belief for a long time that cycling was on the way out, have led to a host of new problems for cyclists as they strive to share roads which were never really designed for them. Add to this an increase in faster and more aggressive driving, and it is scarcely surprising that many people are deterred from cycling by today's road conditions.

Once more, this book makes no excuses for the trends in road design which have led to the current situation. But in the real world there are techniques which cyclists can learn to maximise their safety and reduce to a minimum the problems that they encounter. Such techniques are seldom taught, cyclists usually being advised to do what is often impractical and to avoid difficult locations.

The best way to tackle any difficult problem is to break it down into more manageable parts. For example, although you may share a busy junction with more than a hundred other vehicles, you will rarely have to interact with more than one or two other drivers at any one time. Success in the more difficult manoeuvres comes by tackling each situation step by step and riding to suit the current circumstances, whilst making preparations to your advantage for what follows.

Take heed that these skills are not for the novice. You will need to have practised and mastered all that has been taught so far before progressing to these advanced techniques. A good cadence and sprint speed (see Chapter 2) are particularly useful for carrying out the techniques in this chapter. Having said that, most reasonably agile adult cyclists should be capable of acquiring these skills which, exercised correctly, are much less hazardous than it might at first seem.

Negotiation

The skill of negotiation is crucial to many of the techniques necessary for sharing busy roads if you are to make any sensible progress. It is a skill which requires confidence, both with respect to control of your machine and your relationship with other road users. It is also a skill which is at variance with much of the traditional teaching of how to cycle – far from advising you to keep away from other traffic, it requires that you deliberately seek to integrate with it.

Negotiation recognises that you are the driver of a vehicle with as much right to proceed safely and quickly as any other. It relies upon establishing co-operation between you and other drivers in order to facilitate your progress and to protect you from the dangers which would otherwise threaten you. It makes other drivers want to assist you by appealing directly to a basic human instinct – responding with help when it is specifically requested. In other words, you try to influence the actions of others to your best advantage.

The following example illustrates the use of negotiation when you need to pull out into a moving traffic stream in order to pass an obstruction. Subsequent sections will explain the use of the technique in more complicated circumstances.

Chapter 5 described the basic method of overtaking – reducing your speed in order to await a suitable gap in following traffic, and then pulling out into the space. This is fine on two-lane roads where you have right of way or on lightly trafficked multi-lane roads, but on busier roads where you need to change traffic lanes you could wait a long time before there is a sufficient gap. Instead, you need to negotiate with following drivers to let you in when, strictly, the right of way is not yours.

To do this, move to the right side of your lane well in advance of the obstruction and look behind for a gap in traffic that is slightly longer than average. Apart from giving you more space to manoeuvre, a longer gap often suggests that the driver behind is less hasty and more considerate than others, and therefore more likely to let you in. Unless the gap is long, never try to

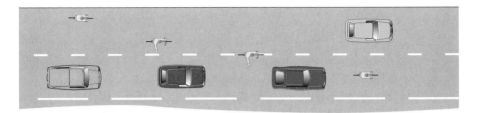

Figure 6.1
Negotiation in overtaking
This diagram shows the sequence of events, but is not to scale.

intercept another two-wheeler, a bus or a lorry, as it might be more difficult for the driver to slow down to give way.

As the gap approaches – if possible, while the previous vehicle is still overtaking you – signal right and move to about 0.5 metres (1.5 feet) to the left of the next moving traffic lane (Figure 6.1). This should be a clear indication to the driver behind that you wish to slip in front, but you have not yet moved to a position which puts you in any great danger.

Next you must decide whether or not the driver is responding to your request, or whether it would be better to try again with someone else. You must make this decision very quickly, for any delay in accepting may result in a change of mind by the driver. In practice, most drivers do respond positively to a clear and confident negotiation request, and typically indicate this by slowing a little to let you in. Listen carefully to the sound of the engine. If the driver is going to let you in, move quickly to inside the new traffic lane – the primary riding position will usually be appropriate while overtaking – and continue with the overtaking procedure. If you can give a friendly 'thank you' wave to the driver, so much the better.

If the person following decides not to let you in, move back to the right side of the previous lane and repeat the whole procedure with someone else. It will usually not be long before someone accedes to your request.

A variation of this technique can be used to start off on a

narrow road where the stream of traffic seems unlikely to cease. In this case, you scoot your cycle to just outside the moving traffic lane, aligning it at about 30° to the traffic flow. Wait for a gap slightly longer than average, signal right and edge forward slightly. If a driver accedes to your request, start off as quickly as you can; otherwise move back.

Complex right turns

When turning right from a busy road, it is not so simple to reach the centre as it was in the case of the simpler right turn described

Figure 6.2
Right turn by negotiation
This diagram is not to scale.

in Chapter 5. Again, you should take stock of following and oncoming traffic at least 100 metres (about 330 feet) before the junction, but when you come to start your movement, you will need to proceed more cautiously and make use of negotiation (Figure 6.2).

Assuming a start from the secondary riding position, select a gap in the traffic slightly longer than average, and signal right. Accompany this with a movement to the right which puts you just on the edge of the moving traffic lane. This movement, to indicate that you are serious about turning, can be reinforced with a determined look back straight at the driver. At this point, the driver will either indicate a willingness to let you move further right or will carry on regardless. If the latter, let this driver pass and try again with someone else. When someone agrees to let you in, move briskly to the centre of the road, taking care that the vehicle which let you in is not being overtaken by someone else. Once more, it is worth giving a courteous 'thank you' signal to drivers who co-operate.

If the first road has more than one lane in your direction, you should adopt the same procedure one lane at a time. **Never try to cross all lanes in one movement in traffic.** When the first driver has agreed to let you in, move to the right side of that lane, but not so far that you can be passed on the inside; it is essential to hold each lane until you can enter the next. Do not let yourself be intimidated. In fact, a driver who has willingly let you in will usually be happy to shield you until you can move further, so long as you do not delay unnecessarily.

Next, look behind for a similar opportunity to enter the second lane and negotiate with a driver to let you in, moving onto the edge of the second moving traffic lane as you signal right. Repeat this procedure until you arrive at the centre of the road. You should allow about 50 metres (about 140 feet) per lane to manoeuvre on multi-lane roads, and bear in mind that traffic may be travelling faster in successive lanes, which will require you to seek longer gaps for crossing. You should also remember that you will need a longer gap in oncoming traffic in order to cross the second part of a dual carriageway. The main requirement is patience. Do not be rushed because a following driver becomes impatient or dashes out, although it can be very useful to seek the cover of another vehicle when making a turn.

A skilled and reasonably agile cyclist should be able to negotiate with traffic in order to make multi-lane right turns as described for traffic speeds up to 64 km/h (about 40 mph). Where speeds are higher or the cyclist is less agile, the technique can still be applied if there are sufficiently long gaps between vehicles and visibility is good. Where circumstances are less favourable, it may be safer to stop on the left side of the road and wait for an interruption in the traffic flow in which to cross. If you do decide to stop in this way, do so a little way short of the junction rather than at it, and engage a low gear so that you can accelerate away quickly. Incidentally, don't think – as many people do – that dismounting to make such turns will necessarily be any safer than riding. A bicycle is a somewhat cumbersome object to wheel across a road, and with the cycle at right angles to traffic you may be more vulnerable in crossing than either a pedestrian or a cyclist riding. Wheeling is also slower than riding, so you will be at risk for longer. Generally, crossing as a pedestrian is only safer where there is a protected crossing.

Roundabouts

Roundabouts can be a considerable source of danger to cyclists. In Britain the chance of a cyclist being involved in a collision at a roundabout is 14 times that for a car driver.

It is important, however, not to overstate the problems of roundabouts for cyclists. Many roundabouts operate safely for both cyclists and other road users, and cyclists, too, can benefit from the ease of movement that roundabouts allow. Unfortunately, it is not always easy to predict which roundabouts will present the greatest danger, for more depends on local circumstances than on any particular facet of roundabout design. Thus a large main road roundabout may sometimes be much less of a problem than a small roundabout in a residential area. Driver temperament and traffic flow (ferocity more than speed) are often the main deciding factors.

Because of the difficulty of categorising roundabouts in terms of danger when cycling, all are treated together in this section. You should aim to gain a general understanding of the problems that may be present so that you may apply the advice as appropriate to individual circumstances. Most of the causes of roundabout collisions are predictable. If you learn to ride in a way which makes conflict less likely, you will find that you can cope with the great majority of roundabouts with very little difficulty.

General considerations

It is helpful to analyse the problems cyclists face when using roundabouts, as this will increase your awareness of where the main hazards lie, and thus enable you to ride in a way that minimises these.

Roundabouts should be safer for everyone, as they reduce the number of conflicting movements compared even with traffic signals, requiring drivers to give attention to traffic from only one direction at a time. Unfortunately, many motorists use the increased safety to allow themselves to drive faster or less carefully, and this can cancel out any benefit to the less well-protected road user. Discipline at roundabouts is often poor.

The biggest danger to cyclists is on the circulating road as you pass an intermediate entry – over 70% of cycle crashes on roundabouts happen at the mouth of an entry road. Frequently, drivers fail to cede your right of way at these places, sometimes because they haven't noticed you.

Good positioning by a cyclist is extremely important at a roundabout, and the following sections will detail the preferred positions for negotiating the different designs. The most important rule to bear in mind when riding around any roundabout is to **keep well clear of the give way markings,** for they depict the zone of greatest danger.

Following on from this is another rule of considerable importance: **always keep away from the outside edge of a roundabout,** no matter which exit you are aiming to take. As well as taking you too close to the danger zone of the give way markings, such a position makes you all the more difficult for drivers to see. At roundabouts in particular, drivers are above all looking out for other motor vehicles. As a cyclist, you are at your safest if you ride where a car would be driven for the same manoeuvre. Near the edge, you may also be masked by signs and lamp-posts, and you are very likely to be cut across dangerously by drivers turning left – another of the most common causes of collision.

Even when you do ride in a similar position to a car, drivers approaching a roundabout can still have difficulty seeing you. This is exacerbated by the very philosophy of a roundabout, which encourages drivers to keep moving as much as possible, reducing the care that they might otherwise take. Designs may also permit a high-speed approach.

In fact, many motorists themselves fear roundabouts, whilst plenty of others find it difficult to cope when there is a lot of traffic or when several main routes converge. Their main concern is to get through the junction as quickly as possible and in one piece. Attention is concentrated on watching out for dangers to themselves (which does not include anything as small as a cycle), controlling their vehicle amidst the complex weaving which often takes place, and finding their way to the correct exit. In addition, drivers often have to make a number of gear changes. That doesn't leave a lot of attention for looking out for other people.

At larger roundabouts the entry roads bend to the left as they meet the circulatory road, sometimes considerably. Circulating vehicles already on the roundabout are therefore often more behind than to the right of a driver approaching the give way line, and this makes it much more difficult to see them. A vehicle as small as a cycle can easily be overlooked (Figure 6.3). At the same time, if the driver is concentrating to the right, it will be harder for that driver simultaneously to monitor traffic in front, such as a cyclist passing the give way lines. Slower cyclists are particularly vulnerable here.

In all these cases, keeping well away from the edge will at least

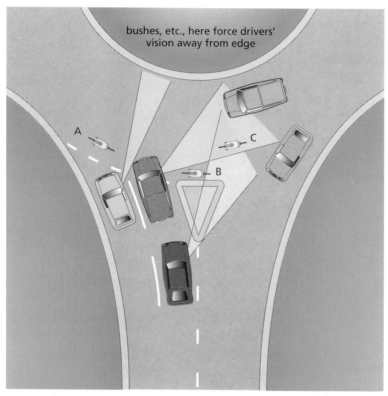

bushes, etc., here force drivers'
vision away from edge

A

C

B

Figure 6.3
Typical arcs of concentration of drivers entering a roundabout
Cyclists A and B are difficult to see and very vulnerable. Cyclist C is
more visible and has greater room for manoeuvre.

give you warning of a driver not ceding right of way, and will
allow a few metres in which you can take avoiding action. But
bear in mind that it will take any driver longer to give way if you
are seen when the driver is accelerating away from the give way
lines than while braking approaching them. Many drivers cannot
move from accelerator to brake quickly. Another way of
avoiding trouble at less busy roundabouts is to pace your riding
so that you don't arrive at an entry road at the same time as
another vehicle. A small adjustment to your speed will be all that
is usually required.

Even if all drivers were perfect, roundabouts would still hold hazards for cyclists. A fundamental rule of braking for any two-wheeler is to avoid doing so on a curve, particularly if the surface is wet or icy. But at roundabouts you have no choice. The entries to main road roundabouts are also some of the main places where large deposits of oil and diesel fuel are to be found, adding to the problems of control. In addition, surface defects are more of a hazard if you are not riding in a straight line. On a roundabout there are many demands on your attention.

At a roundabout, a cycle's inherently poorer acceleration and gear changing mechanisms are at their greatest disadvantage compared with those of cars. You are usually at your safest moving on a roundabout if your speed is high and is as close as possible to that of the other traffic. For this you need to be in a high gear. However, you, as others, should give way to traffic already circulating on the roundabout; at best this will mean slowing, but it may mean stopping. In order to move away again smartly you will need to be in a low gear. As you can't change gear when stationary on a derailleur-geared bicycle, you may face a dilemma as to which gear to use – there is much more uncertainty than at traffic signals.

The answer is to make a judgement of the conditions as you approach the roundabout, based on the traffic flows at the time. If it seems likely that you will be able to move straight onto the circulatory road, perhaps by adjusting your speed slightly to find a gap in traffic, stay in a high gear. If circumstances change, you may then have to make an abrupt stop, but if at all possible keep going and accelerate out of trouble.

If giving way seems likely in advance, approach in a middle gear and more slowly. Make a final judgement when you are about 5 metres (15 feet or so) from the give way line. If clear, accelerate rapidly by increasing your cadence to a rate higher than normal and then change up in gear, if you can.

If a stop is necessary, brake hard until you are only just moving and then change down in gear. So long as you have practised the skill of low-speed riding and gear changing, you should be able to complete this before reaching the line. On roundabouts it is essential that your gears are reliable and correctly adjusted: this is no place to stall.

If at all possible, keep moving, albeit slowly, rather than stopping at a roundabout, so that you will have that much more momentum to proceed when the way ahead is clear. Even with good acceleration, you may find that after a stop, another vehicle has appeared on the circulatory road when you have scarcely crossed the give way line. If possible, you should not stop again having crossed the line, but it is essential to be guided by circumstances – drivers who appear fast from the other side are never to be trusted, although a stern look in their direction can often make them yield, as they should.

Particularly problematic is the situation when the centre island restricts your view, decreasing the warning you have of another vehicle approaching. The theory is that this makes drivers take more care, but too often they simply go fast and take the risk.

Single-lane roundabouts

These small roundabouts are mainly found in residential districts and on other minor roads. They pose few problems for cyclists where traffic flows are light, but on busier roads they can be even more dangerous than some larger types.

The greatest danger is that some drivers race a cyclist to the roundabout, cutting sharply across the cyclist's path in order to enter (Figure 6.4). Drivers often do not realise how great a cyclist's speed can be, and as a result there is often insufficient space to complete the overtaking manoeuvre safely, and the cyclist is put at risk. The likelihood of being overtaken in this way seems to be greater where there is no entry island, but if there is an island and a driver still overtakes, it can act as a further hazard by creating a squeeze point.

The difficulty for a cyclist lies in knowing the intentions of a driver behind. Can you ride normally and comfortably, or should you accelerate or brake in order to prevent or counter a dangerous manoeuvre? Sharing a road where there is a series of

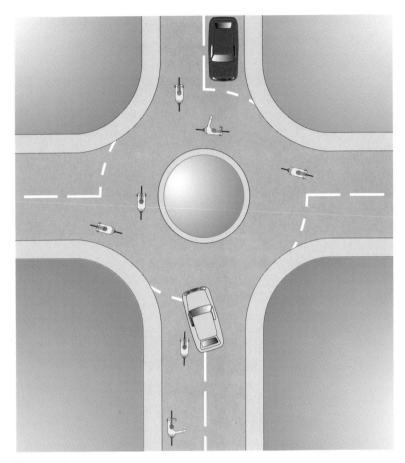

Figure 6.4
A single-lane roundabout
See page 101 for full signalling details.

these roundabouts can be a very strenuous business, even if there's only one car following. Whilst a cyclist can often maintain a near-constant speed, a car will generally be faster between roundabouts but slower through them, and the continuous to and fro between car and cyclist can lead to uncomfortable pressure and a great feeling of vulnerability.

When approaching a single-lane roundabout, take up the primary riding position in good time, and at least 20 metres (60 feet or so) in advance. You should do this whether you are going ahead or turning left or right. You must do your best to dissuade any driver from even contemplating overtaking until you are safely through the junction. If there is following traffic (or if you are unsure), give warning of the move with a short moving-right signal.

If you are going straight ahead, give way to traffic from your right as necessary, and then ride the shortest route through the roundabout. Don't waste time keeping parallel to the edge, but do ensure that no one can pass on either side. A straight course will not only get you out of the roundabout as quickly as possible, it will also be the safest if the surface is slippery or if you need to brake suddenly. If there is traffic coming from the opposite direction or there is a pedestrian nearby, signal left as you approach the exit road, but be cautious about doing this if there is a vehicle close behind, for it can be taken as an invitation to overtake.

For the same reason, if you are turning left, signal your intention only just before you start to make the turn. Always keep in the centre of the lane until you are well out of the roundabout. Some cyclists think that they needn't bother to give way when entering a roundabout if turning left; you must give way, and at small roundabouts it can be especially dangerous not to do so.

When turning right, signal your intentions early, and ensure that this is seen by oncoming drivers. Although you should keep a good distance from the entry roads you pass, you should not get too close to the centre island. This would mean a sharper turn, and might also encourage someone to pass on your left side. A position just to the right of the centre of the circulatory road is usually best, going straight to your exit from opposite the previous entry.

One problem with turning right is the difficulty of maintaining a signal as you turn. It is easy for an oncoming driver not to realise your intentions until you are close in front. The answer is to signal intermittently. Critical times to signal are when entering the roundabout, and as you approach intermediate exits.

Multi-lane roundabouts

These are found on busier roads. As well as having a wider circulatory road, the entries to these roundabouts are often two, three or more lanes wide, at least for the final few metres leading into the roundabout. Although some examples on roads with low traffic speeds pose no great problems, these roundabouts are often a place of great difficulty and danger for cyclists, as a common purpose of their design is to increase junction capacity and keep vehicles moving.

The two principal dangers are traffic entering at intermediate roads, and weaving movements as drivers jostle to get to their desired exit. Once you have entered, you cannot usually go back!

As you approach a roundabout on a busy road, make your presence known early by occupying the primary riding position (Figure 6.5). In general, you should start to do this as soon as you pass the advance 'Roundabout Ahead' sign, but on high-speed roads, where signing distances are greater, wait until you are about 100 metres (about 330 feet) from the junction, though earlier if you are turning right.

If you want to turn left, keep about 2 metres (7 feet or so) from the edge all the way through the roundabout, except if there are three or more entry lanes, in which case you should enter in the centre of the left-hand lane and maintain that distance. As at other left turns, signal if you can, but don't if it might encourage someone to overtake you before it is safe to do so. Make sure that you give way to traffic already circulating.

To go ahead (or to the second exit where the junction is not just a crossroads), on the approach ease gradually to a position to the right side of the left-hand lane, but take care that no one can pass to your left. If there are only two entry lanes, maintain this position up to the give way line. Where there are three lanes, move to the middle of the centre lane, but be wary of the possibility of someone overtaking on your left. Where there are four or more lanes the situation can be very difficult. If in doubt, use the centre of the second lane from the left, but as far as

Figure 6.5
A multi-lane roundabout

possible keep just within the path of other vehicles which appear to be making the same manoeuvre. In any event, try not to get too hemmed in or masked by traffic on either side.

At less busy roundabouts, wait your turn, if necessary, at the give way line in the usual way. On very busy roads, however, you could wait for a long time, whilst the risk to yourself can only increase if you hold up following drivers too long. The answer is to seek the shelter of another vehicle, preferably one that is unlikely to accelerate away too quickly. Buses and lorries are good choices, but watch out that you are not so close to them as to be hit when they turn. Otherwise look for a driver who is not revving the engine or similarly showing impatience.

Once you have entered the roundabout, proceed as quickly as you can, adopting a position to the right side of the left-hand circulatory lane, which may, but will probably not, be marked. This will give you the shortest and quickest ride through the roundabout, and will keep you as far as possible from intermediate entry roads.

Turning right at a multi-lane roundabout (or going beyond the second principal exit where several major roads join) is more difficult, particularly on fast-flowing, heavily-trafficked roads. It needs great care, confidence and, preferably, the ability to attain a sprint speed of about 32 km/h (20 mph). Approach the roundabout in the middle of the right-hand lane, reaching this position by following the same techniques which would be applicable to a conventional right turn from the same road. Normally, you should not leave sufficient room on your right for anyone to pass, but where there is a lot of traffic turning right, it can be advantageous to adopt a position just to their left and to use the shelter of those vehicles for making the turn. Always make the most use of others for protection at any busy roundabout. Once on the circulatory road, ride to the left of the centre of the right-hand lane (whether marked or not) until you are opposite the entry before your exit. Then spiral out of the roundabout in a gradual curve (don't make any sudden turns), finally adopting the primary riding position on the exit road. It is usually best not to signal right on the roundabout, but do signal left clearly before you begin to cycle out of it.

During any roundabout manoeuvre, you must keep your eyes and ears alert, monitoring other traffic all the time. Be ready to respond – with a quick move to the left or right, with braking or acceleration – to the slightest threat to your course. On multi-lane roundabouts, negotiation also has an important role to play in persuading drivers to assist you. The technique is similar to that you would use when wishing to carry out a complex right turn, but at a roundabout you may have to negotiate with drivers on both sides, sometimes at the same time, and the whole procedure needs to be carried out more quickly. As usual, you indicate your intentions by signalling, backed up with a small 'please let me in' movement, completing the move once someone has agreed. Very often a driver who has let you in will continue to protect you, but don't trust anyone else!

Where you pass an entry road, be wary, particularly of traffic in the furthest lanes from you. A closer driver may have seen you and be waiting, but that driver's vehicle may mask you from others. If there is any likelihood of someone moving into your path, move to the right. If you are going to the next exit, signal left as you pass the entry road. This can deter drivers from edging out too far, but be ready to get your hand back quickly to the handlebars.

A final danger point presents itself as you leave many multi-lane roundabouts, at the place where the exit road swings left to follow the normal course of the road. The danger is particularly noticeable when the road reverts to a single lane in each direction, for it is here that the exit lanes usually merge. This relatively sharp deflection can act as a pinch point between drivers accelerating away and a cyclist. Deter drivers from getting too close by keeping well away from the edge, preferably by holding the primary riding position until the hazard is passed.

Mini-roundabouts

A mini-roundabout is one with a flush or slightly raised central marking, but no kerbed island. It may be single- or multi-lane. The mini-roundabout is generally used where there would be

Figure 6.6
A mini-roundabout

insufficient space to install a larger roundabout, and is designed so that large vehicles, which cannot negotiate the sharp turn, may go straight across the centre (Figure 6.6). Generally, mini-roundabouts have a good safety record for cyclists, but this may be in part because they are found on roads of 48 km/h (30 mph) average speed or less.

One problem for cyclists is that cars may also go straight across the central marking. Sometimes they do this at speed, particularly where the roundabout is placed at a T-junction and there is no deflection on the approach. Such a driver may overtake you dangerously on the roundabout.

A second problem with mini-roundabouts is that the width of the circulatory road is often limited, and the give way markings can be very close. There is little warning for a cyclist, particularly when making a right turn, if a driver fails to cede right of way, and correspondingly little room to take avoiding action. Drivers are often confused as to who has right of way at a mini-roundabout.

A further problem you may encounter with turning right at single-lane mini-roundabouts is that, having entered the roundabout, it is not always possible for a cyclist to continue signalling; the turn may be too tight, so both hands are needed on the handlebars. It can happen that a driver approaching fast from the opposite direction does not see an advance signal and so goes ahead, believing the cyclist not to be turning. On these roundabouts, there is very little room for error on anyone's part.

Negotiate a mini-roundabout in the same way as you would an ordinary single- or multi-lane roundabout, but watch out particularly for the problems discussed above. If turning right, select a lower gear to enable you to accelerate away quickly after a sharp turn; give further signals if you stop, when you cross the give way line and before you start to turn. If in doubt, let an erratic driver go first, and be very cautious of large vehicles, which may not be able to stop quickly.

Multiple roundabouts

These comprise two or more roundabouts placed close together and sometimes immediately adjacent to one another. They may be ordinary, mini-, single- or multi-lane roundabouts (Figure 6.7).

At first sight, these junctions appear merely to multiply the difficulties of their composite roundabouts. Whilst this may be so at some locations, and the greatest care always needs to be exercised, at other places the general confusion caused by the complex junctions seems to reduce traffic speeds and leads to greater care by all concerned. Under these circumstances, a cyclist can sometimes move through the roundabouts more easily than other road users.

Another, rarer, type of multiple roundabout is where there is a ring of mini-roundabouts around a large roundabout which can be travelled in either direction. These, too, need to be treated with caution.

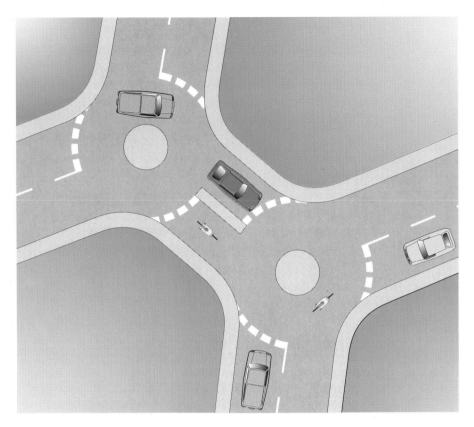

Figure 6.7
Multiple roundabouts

Gyratories

If large roundabouts are difficult for cyclists, gyratory systems can be even more so. In this context, a gyratory means a much enlarged roundabout, with entries and exits flared to facilitate movement (Figure 6.8). Sometimes there are buildings, or even other roads, in the centre. Gyratories are usually to be found on major roads. The circulatory traffic system, comprising just a ring of one-way streets of more or less conventional design, and typical of the type found within older town centres, is much less of a problem, although you must take care to keep to the correct lanes.

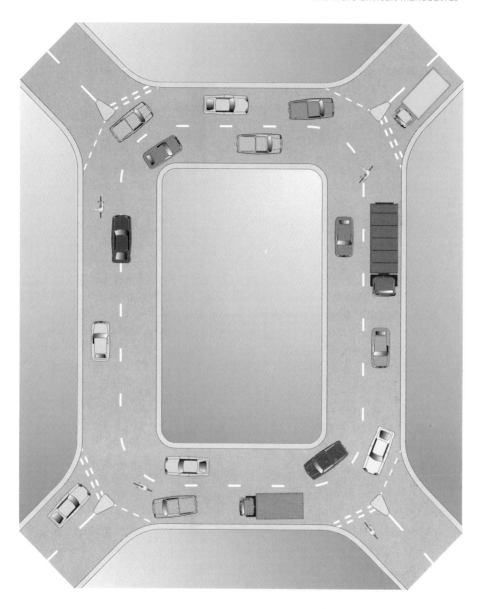

Figure 6.8
A gyratory

The main difference between a gyratory and a roundabout is that with a gyratory, the distance between the converging roads is greater. The same difficulties confront a cyclist approaching a gyratory or riding past intermediate entries as exist at a large roundabout, but there is the added problem of the extra distance to be ridden amidst weaving traffic, which often moves quickly. Whilst taking the first turn left is no great problem, to ride in any other direction will mean that you will need to be in the centre of the road for an appreciable time, with traffic passing on both sides. This can be hair-raising, particularly for the slower rider. Worst times are in moderate traffic flows; when there is a lot of congestion, speeds are usually lower.

It is hard to give general advice on negotiating gyratories, as the difficulties can vary so much from place to place and time to time. As far as possible, you should adopt the same positioning as at a roundabout, but best of all try to spot the actual paths taken by other vehicles going in your direction and ride about 1.5 metres (5 feet) inside that path. If you are going to a minor exit towards which traffic flows are light, use the path to the following exit but veer left early. Take great pains to make your presence obvious to others. Signal right as you approach intermediate exits to emphasise that you are not turning left (you need not actually be going right). Try to 'adopt' a driver to give you shelter for at least the most difficult sections by use of the negotiation technique, but be wary if that driver leaves you.

There may be occasions when it would simply be too hazardous to follow the path taken by other traffic. This applies especially to slower riders, but even the fittest can be in difficulty if the gradient is against them or the road is very wide. Under these circumstances, you may have little option but to follow a route nearer the outside, but to do so demands the greatest care. Except to turn left, do not ride closer than about 3 metres (10 feet) to the edge of a gyratory, and keep well away from give way lines. To cross intermediate exits, it may be best to pull in for a while to await more favourable traffic conditions, or simply to be sure what following vehicles are doing. Remember that restarting will be slow, so allow time for this.

Slip roads

These are found at split-level junctions on trunk and principal roads, and enable traffic to join or leave the main road at high speed. Cyclists going ahead on the main road are at great risk at such junctions, and when crashes do occur they tend to be serious, with a 1 in 20 chance of a fatality.

It is not just the speed of traffic which causes the problems, although this certainly increases the severity of any collision. Drivers on an entry slip road concentrate their attention to the right, in order to select a gap in traffic into which they can merge, and to look out for dangers to themselves. This means that drivers may fail to notice a cyclist crossing ahead, even if he or she has the right of way. At exit slip roads, the dangers are usually less, as at least drivers leaving the major road keep their attention straight ahead.

Having recognised the problems, it is usually not too difficult for cyclists to minimise hazards at slip roads, although it can mean ceding your priority and manoeuvring in a way contrary to the indications of the road markings. This is unfortunate, but the dangers at these locations are otherwise too great. Junctions on this type of road are usually far apart, so you will lose little time overall.

Approaching an entry slip road (Figure 6.9a), direct your attention to the traffic on it. Your aim is to cross that slip road as close as possible to where it meets the main carriageway, and you should seek a gap in traffic sufficiently great to enable you to do this. Don't forget to allow adequately for speeds. If traffic flow is not too great, you should be able to pace your riding in such a way that you can manoeuvre as you cycle across the hatch markings, with little disturbance to your journey. Cross the slip road as quickly as possible, at an angle of about 45° to your direction of travel. There is no need to signal.

Where the slip road is busier, you may have to slow down more, or even stop before crossing the slip road. Unless traffic speeds are unusually low, you should not ride along the main carriageway beyond the hatch markings, even if there's no traffic coming – yet!

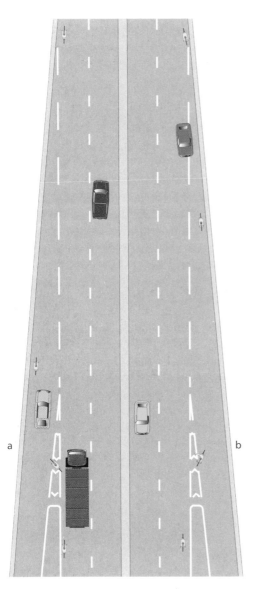

At some entry slip roads, formal cycle crossings are now being marked which follow the same principles, although they often require a sharper turn by the cyclist to cross the slip road at 90°. If traffic flows are high, it may be best to use these, but otherwise the procedure suggested will give similar protection without so much loss of momentum.

Whilst fewer collisions happen at exit slip roads (Figure 6.9b), they are still hazardous places, and it can be difficult to judge the intentions of following drivers. Unless there is no traffic which could arrive in the time it would take you to ride at least 50 metres (about 160 feet) across the mouth, you should join the slip road, riding about 1 metre (3 feet) from the edge, and looking back frequently to observe conditions. Try to pace your riding so that there will be a suitable gap in traffic when you are about 20 metres (60 feet or so) from the junction nose, where you should first signal right clearly, and then move back to the main carriageway as directly as possible. If there is a continuous stream of traffic leaving the main road, you should stop until a suitable gap arrives.

Figure 6.9
Crossing a slip road on a high-speed road
a   entry slip road
b   exit slip road

Free-flow lanes and merges

Like slip roads, free-flow lanes and merges are designed to keep traffic moving at junctions. Although traffic speeds may not be as high as on slip roads, they can still be uncomfortably so for a cyclist.

The commonest places for free-flow lanes are where there is a heavy left-turning movement at a roundabout and at the entry into a one-way street. Merges exist where two main roads converge, one sometimes being a motorway. The idea is that traffic from the left keeps left and that from the right keeps right, without either having to give way to the other at the junction. Weaving movements to sort out subsequent destinations take place further on. The danger for a cyclist coming from the right lies in becoming trapped between the two lanes of traffic and being vulnerable to each (Figure 6.10).

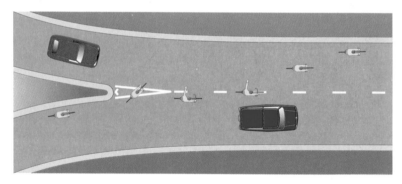

Figure 6.10
Free-flow lanes and merges
If you need to stop, adopt the position of cyclist A.

Unless you want to turn right again soon, you should move to the left side of the road as early as possible, ignoring any 'Keep to Lane' signs. You must do this carefully, for drivers will not necessarily be prepared for your movement, although many will recognise the need for a cyclist to make it. At most traffic speeds, you can negotiate with drivers to let you in, but where speeds are high (e.g., where a motorway joins the main road you are on), the situation is more difficult and you may have to stop until a suitable gap arrives.

Diverges

Diverges exist where a main road splits into two, or sometimes where a motorway begins. One difficult manoeuvre is when a cyclist wants to take the right-hand road, for it is first necessary to cross the left lane(s), in which traffic may be moving fast.

Where possible, start manoeuvring well in advance; a good place is at the end of the zone where other drivers are making similar lane changes. On the other hand, don't manoeuvre too early. During weaving movements, motorists devote a lot of their attention to their rear view mirrors and may not notice you in their path.

Use the negotiation technique to cross each lane in turn, as if making a right turn, ending up at least 1.5 metres (5 feet) inside the first right road lane (Figure 6.11). Do not stay too close to the lane edge, or you will be less visible to a driver who is turning left but who has left it late.

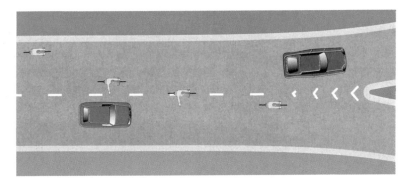

Figure 6.11
Diverges

Under particularly difficult circumstances, you may not be able to cross the left road lane(s), and you will then have to stop and wait for a suitable gap in traffic before proceeding.

Deceleration lanes

These are similar in appearance to exit slip roads, but are provided at junctions on ordinary main roads to allow left-turning vehicles to slow down without impeding the progress of other traffic (Figure 6.12). Although turning vehicles will usually be slowing down, in the presence of a cyclist going ahead, some drivers accelerate first to overtake and then cut in sharply to turn left, braking at the same time. This can result in very little clearance, and much danger for the cyclist.

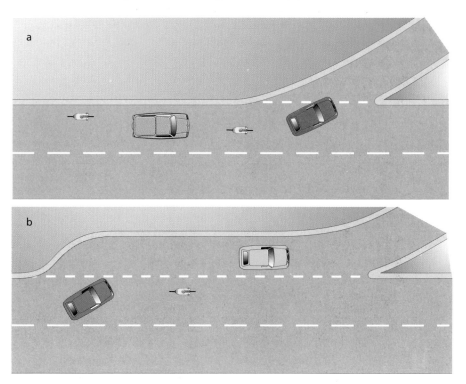

Figure 6.12
Deceleration lanes
a   short
b   long

Some deceleration lanes taper gradually from the major road and are relatively short (Figure 6.12a). These are the ones that give the greatest difficulty. Occupy the primary riding position before the lane commences, and stay there for as long as there is any danger. This will minimise the possibility of drivers overtaking dangerously.

Other deceleration lanes widen into a full-width lane quickly (Figure 6.12b), with the result that drivers can pass a cyclist sooner on the left and do not therefore feel the need to overtake in their haste. As long as you have sufficient confidence to accept vehicles passing on your left, this type of deceleration lane is usually less of a problem.

7 —— Non-traffic hazards

From what you've read so far, it would be easy to think that motor traffic is the only – or at least the greatest – problem for cyclists using the roads. However, as this chapter will show, there are many other hazards to be aware of, and they can be less predictable than a motorist.

Bad surfaces

At best, bad surfaces result in an uncomfortable ride for a cyclist; at worst, they can lead to loss of control, a spill into the path of following traffic, and serious injury. In general, poor road surfaces probably result in more injuries to cyclists and damage to their bikes than any other cause. Bad surfaces include pot-holes, bumps, cracks and trenches in the road. All can be difficult to see in advance, especially when you are riding fast amidst heavy traffic or when the road is wet.

As you ride along, continually scan the surface as far ahead as you can see. Defects are frequently detectable by a change in the colour or texture of the surface. Look out for these, and assume a problem until you are convinced otherwise. Defects are often concentrated along relatively short stretches of road, where the surface is old or where pipes or other services have been renewed; once you encounter one problem, expect others. Road junctions are common places for defects, due to the wear caused by turning vehicles, whilst frequently there is also a build-up of loose debris. It can be difficult dividing your attention between the surface and traffic at busy junctions, but both are a hazard. Develop the habit of scanning the surface as your eyes move from traffic in one direction to traffic in another direction.

If you have sufficient warning of a defect, you can usually avoid it without too much trouble. Alter your course early, being sure to signal clearly to following traffic if you need to pull out. You cannot rely upon motorists to notice surface problems, as they are seldom affected by them. If you need to keep far out for more than a few metres, perhaps because of a long trench, pointing to the problem can help to inform a driver of the reason. As far as possible you should not let pressure from impatient drivers force you onto an uncomfortable or dangerous surface.

Even with very little warning, pot-holes and other small defects can often be avoided by using the technique described in Chapter 2 for avoiding obstacles. However, there will be times when you will have no choice other than to continue straight on. This will always be the case if you have to cross a transverse trench. It is also preferable to go across a pot-hole or bump using the correct technique than to turn sharply to try to miss one, which could put you into the path of following traffic.

To cross a pot-hole, trench or bump with minimum risk to yourself and your bike, you should:

- steer as straight as possible and meet the defect square-on (you will be less likely to be deflected or lose control);

- take your weight off the saddle (to reduce discomfort);

- release the brakes if you applied them previously (to reduce the force on the front forks);

- as you reach the hole or bump, pull up on the handlebars, grasping them firmly.

The last action should result in the bike jumping over the obstacle. When your front wheel has landed on the far side, transfer your weight forward to give the rear wheel a gentler crossing. The whole procedure takes just a second or two to carry out, but needs practice.

Ridges are another hazard. If you must, you can usually mount a 2.5 cm (1 inch) ridge square-on at riding speed, suffering only discomfort, but even a 5 mm (0.2 inch) one will topple you if crossed at too shallow an angle. Ridges are often placed at lay-bys, bus stops and junctions with cycle paths, with little thought of the danger for cyclists. It is useful to learn the effect of different surfaces and edges on your cycle so that you are not caught unawares.

Cobbles and many types of blockwork surfacing are uncomfortable on a cycle, even when newly laid. Vibration can make steering more difficult, whilst bevelled edges or grooves lead to a 'tram-line' effect. They are particularly hazardous when wet or icy. Similar dangers occur where a road is planed prior to resurfacing. If you have to cycle on such surfaces, go slowly and grip the handlebars firmly.

Other bad surfaces cause discomfort and fatigue. General road wear and crumbling are examples, but so is a road recently resurfaced with stone chippings. To minimise discomfort, slow down, reduce your arm and hand pressure on the handlebars, and freewheel from time to time, lifting your weight off the saddle.

Drains and manholes

Drain covers that can trap a cycle wheel are encountered less frequently today than was once the case, but are still to be found in some areas. Don't trust any drain cover with slots parallel to your direction of travel – steer clear.

More commonly, drain and manhole covers are sunk (or occasionally raised) relative to the level of a road. In some cases, the difference in level can be considerable and very dangerous. These are all reasons for keeping at least 0.5 metres (1.5 feet) from the edge of a road and staying alert.

Level crossings

Crossing railway or tram tracks can be particularly hazardous, especially on a cycle with narrow tyres. The smoothness of the rails is in marked contrast to that of a road and can easily cause a spill, whilst the road over a crossing is often uneven.

The most important rule is always to cross the tracks slowly at 90°. Approach a crossing in the primary riding position to deter overtaking, and then look for the smoothest place to cross. If the rails are oblique to the road, either move further out and then turn left to cross at 90°, or move left just before the crossing and then turn right to cross, depending on the direction of the rails (Figure 7.1). Take care to signal your intentions clearly, but return your hands to the handlebars before you cross.

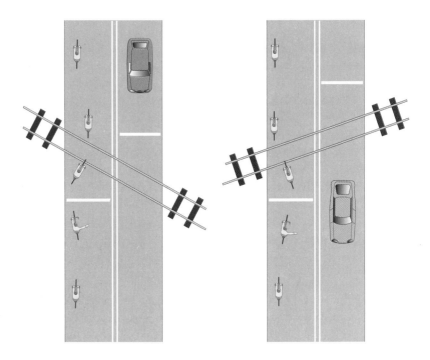

Figure 7.1
Crossing diagonal railway tracks

Camber

Camber is the arched contour of a road surface from one side to the other. The slope on either side is usually less than 5% and poses no problem, but occasionally steeper cambers will be found, particularly close to the kerb. Reverse cambers, where one edge of the road is higher than the centre, may sometimes be encountered, whilst some newer roads are super-elevated on curves, which means that the road slopes steadily from the outside of the curve to the inside.

For a cyclist, steep camber is mainly a problem on bends,

requiring you to lean more when curving right, or less when curving left. If unforeseen, this can result in under- or oversteering, to which the response should be to slow down until the cycle is again under proper control.

When stopping, a steep camber can make it more difficult to set a foot down, possibly leading to a fall. If the camber seems steep, do not ride or stop too close to the road edge, and get off your saddle as you come to a halt.

Slippery surfaces

Surface coverings can reduce grip between wheel and road considerably. Examples include water, mud, oil, ice, leaves and loose gravel. All are worse if the surface is wet, when oil can be difficult to see. Special care is needed on the first wet day after a dry spell. Studs, manhole covers, carriageway markings and zebra crossings may also be slippery when wet.

Whenever slippery surfaces are likely, reduce speed and take extra care turning or braking. Keep your weight low and both hands on the handlebars. If you see a definite hazard, cross it keeping straight and upright, with the brakes off. Changing to a lower gear can help. Going downhill, you will be more stable if you pedal against the brakes.

Pedestrians

All pedestrians are vulnerable, even to a cycle, whilst the elderly and infirm are unable to move quickly. You should show caution, consideration and courtesy towards pedestrians.

However, this can give rise to problems for cyclists. For example, the *Highway Code* requires that all drivers turning at a road junction should give way to pedestrians crossing. Unfortunately, a high proportion of drivers do not, and a cyclist who tries to set an example can well be at risk from others who are less patient. Therefore, the advice must be to give way as far as possible in such situations, but not to do so if it seems likely that following drivers will not.

Approach a zebra or signalled pedestrian crossing in the primary riding position, and be prepared to stop. When stopping, give a slowing-down signal if there is time, and don't restart while anyone is crossing; this only causes unnecessary aggravation. At times a pedestrian who is crossing a wide road will aim to interweave with a cyclist on the far side without making the cyclist give way. Treat such situations with caution, ensuring that no one will be inconvenienced.

All walkers can change direction suddenly and may step out in front of you, but children are particularly unpredictable. Their traffic sense is underdeveloped, whilst a cycle can be difficult for anyone to see or hear. Children may emerge unseen from between parked cars. Wherever there are children alone beside the road, move towards the primary riding position and keep your hands over the brakes. Look out for tell-tale signs of children's presence such as a ball or bicycle nearby, and take extra care near schools, playgrounds and ice-cream vans.

It is illegal to cycle on a footway (or pavement) alongside a road, and you should not do so. In any case, footways are not designed for typical cycling speeds, and riding on them is inevitably more hazardous than on the carriageway.

Other cyclists

Unfortunately, the riding standard of many cyclists is not high, and some are a danger to others as well as to themselves. Children in particular can ride very erratically.

Look out for other cyclists, especially at junctions, where many will put themselves into hazardous positions. If you are turning left from the primary riding position, take care that another cyclist has not come up on your left, intending to go straight on. When overtaking, allow plenty of room, and don't get led into a race by someone who is determined to show how fast they can go. It is better to slow down or stop until that person has gone. Cycle paths are another place for caution: too many cyclists fail to keep left and are not readily seen at night.

Dogs

Dogs may in other ways be man's best friend, but they are a

great hazard to cyclists. Whether just playful or not, dogs on the loose are as likely to cause serious injury to a cyclist as a collision with a car. A fall is likely when a dog runs in front of a cycle, or tries to grab a cyclist's ankles. Dogs seem hypnotically fascinated by revolving legs!

Always be cautious when you see a dog off the lead. In the country, expect to find dogs near farms and houses. Don't just listen out for barking animals: quiet dogs can be just as dangerous and may appear suddenly. If you have warning, get your hands over the brakes and your feet ready to accelerate; it is hard to tell in advance which might be the best action if the dog proves troublesome. Keep going at a steady pace, moving across the road away from the animal if it's safe to do so. Pretend that you're ignoring it – but don't!

If you're chased, you must decide quickly whether you can outpace the animal, or whether it would be better to slow down or stop. All else being equal, it's better to slow down if the dog's ahead of you; otherwise accelerate. To try to placate a dog, ease off pedalling, and speak to it soothingly or shout firmly; either method will work about as often as the other. If the dog is persistent, stop and repeat the technique, edging your bike on. Most dogs submit very quickly.

If you are bitten by a dog, or any other animal, see a doctor quickly. In countries where rabies is rampant, urgent medical attention is essential.

Horses

Horses are easily frightened by cycles, and a frightened horse is a danger to everyone. Ensure that a rider has seen you before you overtake, and allow time for the rider to take firm control of the animal.

Always give a horse plenty of room when you pass (Figure 7.2), even if many motorists don't. If possible, cross right over to the opposite side of narrow roads before overtaking, signalling clearly first right and then left if other vehicles are following. It is better to wait for oncoming cars to pass than to be forced too close to a horse.

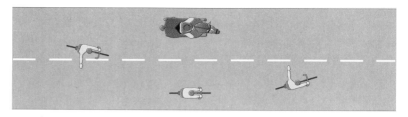

Figure 7.2
Passing a horse

Insects

Although they are such small creatures, insects of one kind or another can cause danger to cyclists. The most likely way is by entering the eye of a cyclist riding along, causing loss of sight of the way ahead. If this happens, keep steering the way you were, and brake quickly. Re-open at least one eye as soon as possible, if only briefly, to get to the side of the road. It helps if you've practised riding blind. Swarms of insects can be a problem at dusk on summer evenings. Wearing spectacles, sunglasses or a peaked cap helps to protect the eyes.

Biting insects can also be a nuisance in some areas, although the draught made by the movement of a bicycle offers some protection. Various insect repellents are available, but their effectiveness varies.

Fumes

Many people worry about cycling in traffic for fear of all the fumes inhaled. Whilst motor fumes are by no means pleasant, doctors consider that the benefits of the exercise obtained by cycling far outweigh the harmful effect of fumes. You are almost certainly better off than a person sitting motionless in a car. However, riding for a long time in dense traffic can lead to drowsiness, and that means you will be less alert than you should be. You must take this into account when manoeuvring.

It is sensible not to breathe in more gases than you must. Don't stay too close to the exhaust pipe of the vehicle in front in queues, and ventilate your lungs well during gaps in traffic. If making a long cross-town journey, use lightly trafficked roads where you can. If you find fumes a problem, you might consider wearing a face mask.

Tiredness

Like fumes, tiredness affects attentiveness: you will be that much slower to recognise and respond to traffic problems. Cycling in the fresh air counteracts tiredness to some extent, but not as much as some people suppose. If you feel tired and you've far to go, you should do something about it.

If your tiredness is mainly the result of physical exhaustion, stopping for a while can help your muscles to renew their strength. Wrapping up warm is also important. Eating a bar of high-energy food such as chocolate is a quick way of topping up your energy reserves.

Mental fatigue is the most dangerous form of tiredness, and is satisfied only by sleep; frequent stops may make you even more tired. Try to find somewhere for an hour's snooze. Alternatively, it may be possible to complete your journey with the assistance of some other mode of transport.

Alcohol and drugs

Apart from the breathalyser regulations, all the laws about driving under the influence of alcohol or drugs apply as much to cyclists as to motorists, and the limits are the same. But the legal limits are to a large extent arbitrary. Any amount of alcohol impairs a cyclist's ability to assess traffic hazards and increases risk, and it is a mistake to think that a drunk cyclist is a liability to no one else.

Many common medicines also affect the ability to react quickly, in a way that could make you more vulnerable. Do not cycle if any of these make you feel drowsy. Only fools mix drinking or drugs with their cycling.

State of mind

The effect on cycling safety when one's mind has been disturbed by some recent event is little appreciated. Examples include an argument or bad news, or, indeed, when elated by good news. Make a special effort at these times to forget everything else and to keep your mind on the road.

8 — Cycling in town

Towns provide a concentration of problems for cyclists, with large flows of traffic and pedestrians, and hazards every few metres. Nevertheless, cycling in towns can be a very practical way of getting about, and it is often the quickest, too.

Most of the techniques described so far apply to cycling in town, but there are also some special considerations.

Choosing routes

The choice of route in a town can make a big difference to how agreeable your journey is. In many instances, of course, there will be no real choice, or time will dictate that the most direct route must be used, but where there are realistic alternatives, bear the following in mind.

The most obvious places to avoid are large roundabouts and gyratories. Ring roads are also a problem, both because they are circuitous and because fast weaving movements by motor traffic are common at junctions. Where major roads must be crossed, try to use light-controlled crossings.

However, contrary to popular opinion, back-street routes are not always safer than main roads. Routes where you frequently have to give way to others destroy momentum, tax your brakes and increase the chances of you suffering from someone's error – perhaps your own. Keep with the priority of other traffic wherever possible.

Narrow roads lined by parked cars should be considered a hazard, as should shopping streets. On the other hand, main roads with bus lanes which cyclists can use are often good routes, while major dual carriageways where parking is prohibited can be easier for cycling than many people imagine, although this depends very much upon the design of junctions.

Traffic-jamming and filtering

'Traffic-jamming' (negotiating traffic jams) is an advanced technique, the basis of which is the fact that cycles are more manoeuvrable than motor vehicles, and that cycles can often proceed in congested streets when other vehicles cannot. Traffic-jamming recognises the different characteristics of cycles and motor vehicles and takes advantage of these to enhance a cyclist's progress and safety. It does not condone illegal or anti-social practices. Skilled traffic-jamming is safe as well as useful, acknowledging the responsibilities of cyclists and inconveniencing no one.

The underlying principle of traffic-jamming is to conserve momentum by stopping as infrequently as possible. Whilst peak speeds of cars are higher than those of cycles, traffic in town tends simply to rush from one jam to another, and overall speeds are low. By maintaining a more constant velocity, cyclists can often achieve a higher average speed than others.

There are three components to successful traffic-jamming:

- correct positioning in moving traffic in order to maintain progress and to maximise safety;

- looking ahead to avoid unnecessary stops;

- passing stationary traffic.

Where your average speed is similar to that of other traffic, correct positioning means adopting the primary riding position. Whilst you should not unreasonably impede others, don't move to the secondary riding position, even if safe to do so, if this would merely lead to leapfrogging.

To accelerate from stops quickly and keep up with the flow, a high cadence and frequent gear changing are advantages. Use a low gear for quick starts, and then a higher gear to maintain position. Good brakes are essential, as traffic often stops abruptly or cuts in front. You must have absolute confidence in the reliability of your cycle. When stopping in traffic, brake hard if conditions permit, in order to give yourself time to change down in gear.

In order to stop as infrequently as possible, keep looking ahead, anticipating the movement of traffic and the changing of traffic lights and other controls. Modify your speed so as to arrive at restrictions when conditions are in your favour, but be careful that slowing down does not encourage someone else to cut in.

It is unreasonable to expect cyclists to wait in long queues of traffic when there is room for them to pass, but filtering through traffic requires great care. Advantages in saving time must be balanced against increased vulnerability while filtering. Normally, overtaking should only take place on the right, and this should be your preference. But on congested roads where there is insufficient clearance from oncoming vehicles, or where there is more than one lane in your direction, this is usually impractical, and it is acceptable to pass to the left – a process sometimes referred to as 'undertaking', and not without reason!

The obvious dangers are that you will be squeezed if drivers move left, that a door will open into your path, or that you will hit pedestrians crossing when they expect no one to be moving. For these reasons **never filter past traffic which is moving faster than walking pace**, and **never pass along the left side of a long vehicle or bus unless there is plenty of space and you are certain that it will not move in the time it will take you to pass.** On multi-lane roads it can be safer to pass between lanes, riding the lane line. Wherever you ride, move slowly in a low gear, ready for an emergency stop should someone step into your path.

Probably the most controversial aspect of filtering by cyclists is behaviour at junctions. Many cyclists continue to pass other vehicles until they are at the head of the queue, even passing the stop line at traffic signals. Although this can mean that the cyclist is better seen once in front of other traffic, and has an advantage in starting, it brings additional dangers. It is always hazardous to be too far to the left when approaching a junction: cyclists who do this can make it difficult for drivers to notice them. The practice also annoys many drivers and pedestrians, for it complicates the traffic situation.

It is much better to stop behind the first vehicle in a queue, allowing that driver to concentrate on choosing a safe moment to move. If possible, adopt the primary riding position, but in any event ensure that the next driver has seen you and will allow you priority. If you are first in a queue, always adopt the primary riding position, and if you are only one or two vehicles back, it is often better to wait in this position, too.

At some junctions, advanced stop lines are being introduced to enable cyclists to go ahead of other vehicles. These are described in Chapter 10.

One-way streets

These vary in width and purpose. In narrow streets, typical of older town centres, the usual rules for cycling apply. Where there is only a single moving traffic lane, normally you should ride in the centre of that lane, well away from parked vehicles, their opening doors and any pedestrians who may step out between them. Retain this position to turn left or right.

Wider one-way streets often form the arteries of an area-wide traffic management scheme intended to speed traffic movement by simplifying junctions and reducing conflicting movements. Here problems can arise for cyclists who need to cross from one side to the other of such a street, to turn to or from the right, or to go ahead where the main flow turns left. Negotiation can be used, but it is often simpler to use the gaps in traffic, when they occur, to change sides in advance of where you wish to turn, and to ride on the right side of the road in the interim. Likewise, it can be easier and quicker to turn right onto the right side of such a road, only crossing to the left when it is clear to do so.

Gaining confidence in riding on the right is a useful skill for towns – and for holidays abroad! There are still primary and secondary riding positions, but these are mirror images of the left-side positions. Do not ride further right than it is safe to do so. If you understand the underlying principles, you should have no problems. It is necessary to be able to look over your left shoulder at traffic behind, and you need to have practised riding with only the right hand on the handlebars whilst doing so.

The only great danger when riding on the right side of one-way streets is where drivers have become accustomed to regarding the right lane as one for fast overtaking. This is most likely where there is a long distance between right turns and where a one-way system resembles a gyratory. You must be guided by local conditions, but prominent positioning will always maximise your safety.

Try to avoid weaving across one-way streets unnecessarily. For instance, if making consecutive right turns, stay on the right in between.

Shopping streets

Streets crowded with shoppers are always hazardous places for pedestrians and traffic alike. It is not simply that there are a lot of people around, but that their movements are erratic and in all directions, including across the road. The greatest danger is from pedestrians stepping onto the road without warning, but drivers will also have their attention distracted. In any crowded street, keep well out from the pavement, with your hands over the brake levers, poised for immediate action. Do your best to ignore the shops and their wares, and keep your eyes scanning constantly from left to ahead to right and back again. Never creep along the kerb where there is little space, even in stationary traffic, for pedestrians will be mainly looking for larger vehicles, and the chance of a collision with someone crossing the road is high. Likewise, drivers will be concentrating on the pedestrians and traffic ahead, and may restart without noticing a cyclist alongside.

If, despite all your vigilance, someone does dart in front of you without warning, brake hard if you can, but keep steering straight. It might sound harsh, but you are better off colliding with a pedestrian than turning under the wheels of a car.

Bus lanes

Bus lanes can be very useful for cyclists, who may use nearly all with-flow and many contra-flow lanes. Cyclists may also use some bus-only streets. Local signs will indicate where cycles are permitted, as well as detailing restricted hours of operation.

The obvious advantage of using a bus lane is that you gain some separation from general traffic, sharing space with the relatively skilled bus drivers, and you may have a clearer passage through a congested street. With contra-flow lanes, you may save a considerable distance by avoiding a circuitous detour. In fact, you should think of all bus lanes mainly as a time or distance saver; the safety benefits in practice are usually minimal. Indeed, access to and from some lanes can require special care if you need to make what for traffic as a whole is an unusual, and therefore less expected, manoeuvre. Be careful with positioning and signalling to make it quite clear where you are going.

When riding in a bus lane, keep to its centre, unless there is another authorised user behind you and it is safe to be passed. Buses should normally overtake a cyclist by straddling the lane line. Take particular care where bus lanes cross side roads, in case drivers cut across you to turn left. Look out, too, for the illegal use of bus lanes by unauthorised vehicles trying to jump a queue of traffic; they may not be looking out for a cyclist.

Traffic calming

In many towns, traffic calming measures and vehicle restricted areas are being introduced to mitigate the impact of traffic, and in particular to reduce vehicle speeds. By reducing the speed, dominance and possibly volume of motor vehicles, these schemes should benefit cyclists. In practice, however, the situation is not so simple, for some of the measures introduce new hazards which can partly or completely negate any advantage gained.

The following sections describe some of the more common traffic calming techniques and their implications for cyclists.

Width restrictions

Traffic throttles, centre islands and chicanes are typical forms of width restriction which are intended to slow traffic, or provide easier crossing places for pedestrians, or both.

In practice, the effect on vehicle speeds can be minimal unless combined with some form of vertical deflection. The effect on cyclists, though, may be significant. Above all else, cyclists need space – for manoeuvring, to give warning of the actions of

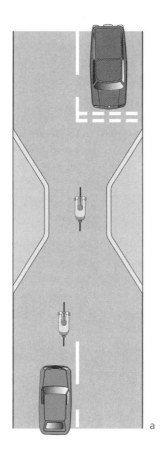 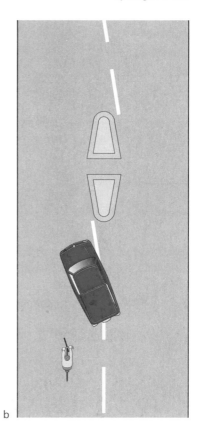

a   b

Figure 8.1
Width restrictions
a   Traffic throttle. Always use the primary riding position.
b   Centre islands. Be aware that drivers may cut in.

others, and in which to take avoiding action should this be necessary. Width restrictions reduce the amount of space available and may endanger a cyclist if a motorist tries to overtake in the limited room remaining.

At traffic throttles (Figure 8.1a), a cyclist can usually take protective action quite easily by adopting the primary riding position at the approach to the restriction. This will mean the cyclist moving close to the centre of the road, and other drivers will then usually stay behind. Signal clearly as you change position, obey the priority signs and keep to the centre of the throttle so that oncoming traffic gives way. Never be tempted yourself to squeeze through any width restriction when traffic is coming towards you.

Centre islands (Figure 8.1b) can be much more difficult, and those with narrow lanes are some of the most potentially dangerous features to be found on the roads today. Here, too, you should adopt the primary riding position at the approach, but be ready for the driver who overtakes regardless and then pulls in sharply left to pass the island. Signalling right can sometimes assert your right of way, but you must always be prepared to move left quickly and hold on.

A chicane is similar to a throttle or centre islands, depending upon whether the entry is situated centrally on the road or to one side. Speeds may be lower due to the zigzag path that vehicles must take.

Some width restrictions include cycle by-pass lanes, the use of which by cyclists is optional. Use these if they would give you an easier passage, but take care that they don't introduce hazards of their own. Narrowness, poor surfaces and drainage covers are typical problems. You may also lose your priority in the traffic stream.

Road humps and cushions

Because the inherent suspension system of a cycle is much less effective than that of a car, a cyclist crossing a road hump experiences more discomfort than a motorist at the same speed. There are dangers, too, if there is a vertical step or upstand to mount, or where the surface has become worn or is slippery. Crossing any upstand also accelerates cycle headset wear. On private roads, some very abrupt humps are to be found which require great care.

Road humps should always be approached in the primary riding position to deter overtaking by another driver. Lift your weight off the saddle at each transition to minimise bike shock and discomfort.

Figure 8.2
Speed cushions

Speed cushions (Figure 8.2) are a variant of a road hump, designed to affect cars but not wider vehicles, such as buses. Instead of extending from kerb to kerb, the raised area is of limited width, the normal road surface being retained on either side. As well as benefiting buses, speed cushions overcome many of the problems of road humps for cyclists, who may ride between the cushions.

You should approach speed cushions in the primary riding position, moving left as you reach the cushion. Return to an appropriate riding position immediately afterwards.

Surface treatments

Non-tarmac surfaces are often used in traffic calming schemes to delimit carriageway space, to encourage low speeds or simply for visual appeal. Whilst some of these treatments have no special effect on cycles, others lead to discomfort and can affect cycle control. Cobbles and some kinds of blockwork are examples. In all cases, lift your weight off the saddle to minimise discomfort, and hold firmly on the handlebars. Take particular care when it is wet or icy.

Rumble strips of coarse chippings, setts or thermoplastic material, laid transversely across the road, also affect cycle control, sometimes markedly. They can be very dangerous if crossed at speed. Sometimes it will be possible to pass by the side; if this is not possible, hold tight, proceed slowly and use the primary riding position to deter overtaking.

Environmental areas

In some localities, whole areas have been 'traffic calmed' or closed to through motor traffic by road closures and other measures.

As long as reasonably direct through routes for cyclists remain – such as the provision of cycle exemption gaps at road closures – environmental areas can be useful for cycling, with the usual caveats that any route should have good surfaces and be reasonably free from dense parking and junctions at which you must give way. On the other hand, if through routes are circuitous, there is no reason – and usually little safety benefit – why cyclists should prefer these to more direct roads.

However effective restrictions may be in reducing speeds at particular places, one result is that drivers spend more of their time accelerating and braking while driving along such roads. One consequence of this is that even good drivers may have their attention distracted from the road, whilst some drivers react in such a way as to minimise the effect of the restrictions on their progress. To a cyclist, fierce acceleration and braking by modern cars causes more discomfort and danger than absolute speed. For this reason alone, many experienced cyclists prefer free-flowing main roads to the 'dodgems' problems of some environmental areas. The use by cyclists of roads such as these for through journeys is generally only preferable where the lengths are short and they enable major hazards to be avoided or quiet routes to be linked.

9 — Cycling in the country

In the countryside, cycling becomes a real pleasure, and you can enjoy the peace and tranquillity of your surroundings in a way that no other driver can. But even in the heart of the country there are problems to contend with and new skills to acquire, and whilst crashes are less frequent on country roads than in town, when they do occur they tend to be more severe.

Choosing routes

Roads in the countryside tend to divide between two extremes. The majority of roads offer peaceful riding over considerable distances. Seek particularly the unclassified roads, which are coloured yellow on Ordnance Survey 1:50,000 maps. There are few parts of the country where these roads cannot be joined together to form very satisfactory routes for the cycle tourist; for the most peaceful routes, keep clear of large towns and industrial areas and give preference to the narrower lanes.

Major roads, on the other hand, and particularly trunk routes (suffixed 'T' on maps), can be very busy with large numbers of heavy lorries. Speeds are often very fast, and drivers do not expect to meet cyclists. Busy roads which are narrow can be especially hazardous. If you are riding in the country simply to get from place to place as quickly as possible, you might have to use these roads, as indeed you might in order to enter a town that you wish to visit. Wherever possible, however, try to avoid them. As in towns, dual carriageway trunk roads are usually better for cycling than single carriageways, as drivers will have more room to give you the clearance they should when overtaking.

Often, one consideration in choosing country routes is the hilliness of the terrain. Don't be misled by the folklore that cycling is easiest on the flat: you pedal for longer where there are no descents to freewheel, and fatigue is experienced sooner. Gently undulating roads are much the least tiring overall, as well as being more interesting. In windy weather, it is often better to seek the shelter of hills or a winding, narrow lane than to use a flatter or more direct, open road, even if this means taking a slightly longer route.

Narrow lanes

To a large extent, the width of a road reflects the amount of traffic using it, so it is not surprising that cyclists cherish riding along narrow country lanes. They are also the one place where a cycle is more clearly the equal of other vehicles, for it is no longer so easy to pass or ignore.

Narrow lanes can be travelled by four-wheeled vehicles in only one direction at a time, and passing places, often informal, are to be found every so often. Sometimes there is sufficient room in between for a car to pass a cyclist safely, but if not, you shouldn't hesitate to keep to the centre of the road until a passing place is reached. If you meet a car coming towards you, keep in the centre until the driver has slowed right down, and then pass as best you can to the left side. If you meet a lorry coming the other way, even a cycle may not be able to pass, and you may have to retrace your path to the previous passing place.

The centre of the road should be your preferred riding position along narrow country lanes, but in practice the surface will often be unsuitable and you will need to keep further left. However, you should alter your position to best advantage as necessary. For instance, approaching a left-hand bend, ride on the right side to maximise visibility; similarly, for a right-hand bend, ride on the left. All the time keep listening for other vehicles, and be sure to return to the left side of the road at widenings and junctions.

Bends on country roads

Many country roads twist and turn around sharp bends, with restricted visibility. Drivers familiar with the roads sometimes travel much faster than they should, and if cycling is not common in the locality, they may not be at all prepared to expect a cyclist. Whenever you ride through bends on roads of this type, keep to the primary riding position.

Long hills

In the country, hills are frequently a mile or more long, and in mountainous areas they may be considerably longer. The physical skills of hill climbing were discussed in Chapter 2, but if you are going to spend some considerable time climbing a hill it is also necessary to be prepared psychologically. From this point of view, the hardest part of a hill is the beginning, while you strive to find the gear best suited to the gradient. Having found that, you can relax more, admire the scenery and forget the pedalling; it soon becomes automatic! Long uphills can be strenuous, but the exhilaration of reaching the summit entirely by your own power cannot be matched by any other form of travel and makes it all worthwhile.

The technique of zigzagging up or down a hill when there is no other traffic has been mentioned. At the approach to mountain passes, very often the road itself will zigzag, with sharp hairpin bends at the changes of direction. The insides of these bends are sometimes of a much steeper gradient than the road before and after, and the camber can be unfavourable. Always adopt the primary riding position approaching a hairpin bend, signalling clearly if you intend to take the bend wide (Figure 9.1). Be alert to traffic from the opposite direction cutting the corner. If there

Figure 9.1
Hairpin bends
When negotiating hairpin bends on mountainous roads – whether going up or down – take the bend wide.

is no other traffic and visibility is good, it can be advantageous to cross to the outside of a steep bend.

One of the greatest joys of cycling is that of descending a long hill. It is in many ways the just reward for the effort of the last climb up, whilst part of that joy is undoubtedly the thrill of freewheeling at speed. In many places in the country this experience can be enjoyed quite harmlessly, but it must always be borne in mind that speed increases danger, and you should pay full attention to the cautions given in Chapter 2 about descending hills.

Farms

Farms are the livelihood of the countryside, and fascinating places to observe. Many of the lanes preferred by cyclists pass right by farmyards, which provide a close insight into farm life. However, farms can present hazards, too: slow down when approaching one, and take care.

Mud on the road is a characteristic of farmyards and field entrances away from the principal traffic routes, as is dung from farm animals. At best this can coat a cycle in a brown slurry; at worst it can cause a fall under less than pleasant circumstances. Frequently, road surfaces past farms are damaged; mud over the pot-holes and ruts can increase the chance of a fall.

Always look out for animals near farms. Larger ones such as cows and sheep are usually no great problem, although not to be argued with! If they are being herded along the road, don't try to pass to the side: you may be crushed or splattered. It's better to wait if they're going in your direction, or to retreat if they're coming towards you. Do follow the directions of farmers herding cattle.

Smaller creatures such as chickens, geese and ducks can be more of a problem. They will usually try to get out of your way (although geese may be more aggressive), but in doing so they may take the most direct route past your front wheel.

Dogs are frequently to be found in farmyards, and the usual cautions apply (see Chapter 7).

Vegetation

Trees and hedges by the roadside contribute much to the country scene, and can also have important advantages in reducing the effect of wind on a cyclist. However, such vegetation also causes problems. One is that close hedges reduce forward visibility, not only for yourself but also for anyone coming towards you. On roads of this kind you must be particularly attentive at bends and near junctions of any kind. Sensible positioning and keen listening are important.

Another danger is caused by twigs or thin branches lying on the road. These can be picked up by a cycle wheel, and then become stuck at the mudguard stays. In extreme cases this may cause the mudguard to collapse into the wheel, but in any event there is the possibility of the wheel stopping abruptly and of the rider being thrown over the handlebars. Take great care to avoid debris of this kind on the road, and slow down as necessary.

Low, overhanging branches from trees and unchecked growth from hedges can also prove a danger, especially if at head height. Remember that a cyclist's head is higher than the roof of the average car, so clearance is not guaranteed just because other traffic uses a road. Thin branches without leaves can be very difficult to see.

Less dangerous, but very much a nuisance, are punctures due to thorns on the road. These can occur anywhere, particularly in autumn, but are most often a problem where roadside hedges have been cut recently. Keep your eyes open for signs of trimming, and then avoid remnants on the road as best you can. If you have to pass hedge trimming in progress, have patience, move to the opposite side of the road and ride carefully. It can be useful to stop just afterwards to remove any partially embedded thorns from your tyres before they can penetrate further.

Cattle grids

These are commonly encountered in farming areas, often replacing gates at farm boundaries and along unfenced roads. Although a well-designed and maintained cattle grid poses no problems for cyclists, the same is certainly not true of grids where rails are missing or bent, where the spacing is too wide or where the road surface on either side is uneven. Even those grids which are not unsafe differ considerably in the discomfort they inflict on a cyclist, whilst all grids are hazardous when wet or icy.

There are conflicting requirements for the speed at which a cyclist should approach a cattle grid. Generally, the faster you cross, the less discomfort you will feel. However, if there is something dangerous about the grid, approaching too fast will not allow you time to take evasive action. Therefore, the advice must be to approach cautiously, looking carefully at the surface. As soon as you can see that it is safe, accelerate. Unless you are going uphill, you should freewheel across the grid itself, holding tightly to the handlebars to counter the vibration produced by the rails. At the same time it is important to lift your weight off the saddle in order to minimise the force of the rail and road edges on the wheels.

Never follow too close behind another vehicle crossing a cattle grid in case it slows down more than you have anticipated. Use the primary riding position to deter anyone from overtaking. It is usually possible to pass unsafe cattle grids by an adjacent gate.

Fords

Like cattle grids, fords are another form of barrier through which country lanes pass directly. They, too, pose hazards which can cause a spill, but many cyclists find fords fascinating and delight in 'ford bashing' by riding through them whenever possible!

Three factors need to be considered before crossing a ford, and it pays to inspect the site first:

- The water should not be too deep; 15 cm (6 inches) or so is about the maximum that can be negotiated easily, as the force of water against the wheels can be considerable. If the water is more than about 5 cm (2 inches) deep you will get your feet wet! There is usually a depth post adjacent to a deep ford.

- The water should not be flowing too fast. If it is, the cross current may be sufficient to alter your course, particularly where a ford is wide.

- Look carefully at the road surface beneath the ford. If it is loose or uneven, you may skid or a wheel may get caught. And if there is any algae (green slime), the surface will probably be very slippery and not at all suitable for wet cycle tyres.

If all seems well, select a low gear and ride through the ford on a straight course, pedalling all the time. Sometimes the road will dip into and out of the water, so be prepared for sudden changes of inclination.

If you decide not to ride through a ford, there will usually be a footbridge close by.

Ferries

Cyclists can use most pedestrian ferries, as well as all vehicle ones. To use the former means carrying your cycle on board, and this is easier if you remove the luggage first. You should also remove the pump and anything else that might drop off or fall in the water between boat and shore! As most pedestrian ferry journeys are short, it is best to stay with your bike to make sure that it doesn't fall. Holding the brakes on can help to keep both the bike and yourself still. If the crossing is rough and the cycle is not under cover, try to protect it as best you can from salt water spray.

Although there remain a few crane-loaded car ferries, most are now of the roll-on, roll-off type. Cyclists should use the normal vehicle entry, riding on and off. When doing so, select a low gear, even if the loading ramp goes down. There will often be a short, steep hump where the loading ramp meets the ship, for which a low gear may be necessary, and in any case the exit on the far side of the crossing may well rise steeply.

Loading ramps and ship decks are wet and often slippery, and sometimes there is cross-ribbing on the surface which can affect steering control. You should keep a tight hold of the handlebars while entering and leaving a ship, and gear changing is inadvisable. Ride in the centre of the loading ramp if possible, for it would be dangerous for another vehicle to overtake. Keep your eyes open for slots or other hazards, steering as straight a line as you can.

Off-road routes

Ordinary roads are not the only places where cyclists may ride in the countryside. Cyclists have a legal right to use bridleways (but must give way to horse riders and walkers), byways and routes marked on Ordnance Survey maps as 'road used as a public path' (RUPP). In Scotland, but not England and Wales, cyclists may also use cross-country footpaths.

In addition, there are country lanes which have not been metalled but which are, nevertheless, available for anyone to use. These are often referred to as 'white roads', because of their colour on OS maps, although this does not mean that all uncoloured roads shown on a map are public roads. It can be difficult to tell which are which, but it is usually reasonable to assume that a road is public if other defined rights of way, such as footpaths and bridleways, terminate on it.

Finally, there are a number of routes in the country which cyclists are permitted to use, but which are not necessarily rights of way and on which, occasionally, a toll may be payable or a permit required. Examples include routes through forests and country parks, cycle/walking trails along old railway lines, canal towpaths and private roads.

Although some of these routes may be tarmacked, in the majority of cases surfaces will be rough and quite unsuited to fast riding. They may also be subject to considerable variation in condition, depending upon recent weather. Many bridleways and RUPPs are quite unrideable at any time (cyclists may use them, but they are only maintained in a condition suitable for horses), and it can be a real challenge to wheel or carry a cycle through a quagmire! The better paths are often those shown on a map as fenced.

These routes, then, are seldom time savers, but for the cycle tourist with time to explore, they can offer very peaceful and traffic-free penetration into the heart of the countryside. In some parts of the country there are long-distance bridleways and 'rough-stuff' routes, which can take several days to cover by cycle.

Cycling along the easier routes – such as those publicised as cycle trails (see Chapter 10) – will probably require a lower gear than for on-road cycling, and you may have to endure the lesser comfort of a poor surface, but at a leisurely speed there should not be too many difficulties. Loose surfaces, pot-holes, bumps and mud are likely to be the greatest hazards to look out for.

Riding rougher tracks, on the other hand, is a much more skilful business and needs to be treated seriously. The potential for losing control is always high, and it would be no joke to be stranded a mile or more from the nearest road with a broken leg or even a buckled wheel. You must have complete mastery of your machine, good judgement of surfaces, and the ability to react quickly to sudden changes in conditions. You must also be able to recognise the point at which you should get off and walk.

There are two essentials of a bike for rough riding: very low gears, and a front fork rake such that your feet (with toe clips) cannot hit the front mudguard. All-terrain bikes have the advantage of being more robust, with wide tyres affording better grip, and no mudguards to clog up.

Two rules of riding are: always keep firm hold of the handlebars, with your hands over the brake levers, even if climbing a hill, and keep your feet on the pedals (toe clips are an asset here). Keeping your body low and weight off the saddle will maximise stability and comfort. You should realise that rough riding is hard work mentally as well as physically and demands your continuous attention. If you want to admire the scenery, always stop in order to do so.

Because of the need for firm steering control, gear changing is not easy when riding a rough path. Always engage a low gear before the going gets too rough, preferably a very low gear, and then keep to it, increasing your cadence to compensate where the going is easier.

Keep your eyes fixed on the path ahead, concentrating on the zone 1–5 metres (3–15 feet or so) beyond your front wheel. Look out for rocks and holes in the path and other hazards. Plan your course quickly but carefully to the limit of the zone. Especially with narrow tyres, don't try to go over any loose material that's bigger than a cherry; it will probably slip from under you. Be careful, too, on inclined surfaces: you may skid.

Steer the front wheel firmly to miss obstacles, taking particular care not to hit the gear mechanism, cranks, pedals or your ankles on anything hard. Shuffle the pedals and pump the brakes on and off if necessary to achieve this. Continually keep your eyes open for somewhere to put a foot down. Choose your course so that you steer straight for about a metre after any narrow gap or ridge to ensure that the rear wheel follows. Going downhill, keep the brakes applied and proceed very, very slowly. Descending rough hills is often more difficult and hazardous than climbing them. Where a path dips into a gulley or hollow, ease the cycle down by careful use of the brakes, then quickly accelerate to climb back out. Precise steering control and prudent use of the brakes and pedals are the principal skills of rough riding.

Where there is a choice, ride on firm earth or grass rather than stones, rock or mud. Never try to ride through sand or shingle. Mud and peat can quickly accumulate if the bike has mudguards, stopping the wheels from turning. On paths which are generally firm, if muddy, puddles are usually shallow and can be ridden through. Paths used by farm vehicles often have puddles in deep ruts which need to be avoided. Fords on tracks with stone surfaces may well topple you; you can sometimes use your cycle as a pivot to vault across narrow streams. Wet rocks should always be treated cautiously; bare chalk in particular becomes very slippery and should be avoided. If there are many large rocks in the path, it will probably be better to walk.

Always have respect for the countryside across which you ride, and do your best not to cause damage or to erode surfaces.

Long rides

In terms of distance, what constitutes a 'long ride' will vary from cyclist to cyclist. Most people of reasonable fitness should be able to cover about 80–110 km (50–70 miles) in a day – but not on their first outing! As with any physical activity, cycling gets easier with regular practice. About 160 km (100 miles) in a day is the upper limit for experienced cycle tourists, but more sports-orientated riders might double that.

For the purposes of this section, a 'long ride' means simply a ride which is long for the person making it, whether it is 140 km (about 90 miles) or 50 km (about 30 miles). It also includes shorter rides which need, for some reason, to be made unusually quickly. What is significant in all cases is that you will be riding close to your limits, and you must therefore take care not to overstretch yourself. Think about this carefully when planning such a ride, remembering to make sufficient allowance for the hilliness of the terrain and the possibility of adverse weather, especially a wind not in your favour.

The first thing to remember on a long ride is that you should not exhaust yourself early by riding too fast. Climbing steep hills may seem deceptively easy at the beginning of a day, but this could be counterbalanced by the earlier onset of fatigue later on. It is best to take things easily and to make good use of low gears.

Common discomforts brought on by riding continuously for a long time are numbness of bottom and hands. Changing your position on the saddle from time to time will help relieve the former, and it is often refreshing to lift your weight off the saddle when descending hills and when surfaces are rough. Hand and arm fatigue can be reduced with dropped handlebars by changing hand positions from time to time. In the country, away from traffic, you can take advantage of the alternative positions further from the brakes. Wearing gloves, cycling mittens or using cushioned handlebar coverings also helps.

On any long ride it is best to stop as infrequently as possible and try not to make a major stop until you have covered at least half of the total distance. Although short stops from time to time can be useful for regaining energy, each successive stop will replenish you less than the previous one, and you will subsequently tire more quickly.

Whenever you are riding close to the limits of your capabilities, make sure that you are carrying some high-energy food, such as chocolate, and sufficient money in case you have to curtail your journey and travel by other means. It is best to eat little and often when cycling, and in the country you can frequently do this while riding along. Do not wait until you are too weak or feel cramp before you replenish your energy. You should make one or two stops of about an hour each during a full day's riding, allowing you to eat a proper meal and regain your strength. But make sure that you have digested well before restarting, and then be wary of drowsiness impairing your attention. Fortunately, for a cyclist in the fresh air, this effect usually passes quickly.

10 — Cycle paths and other facilities

Most people believe that the segregation of cyclists from other traffic by the provision of cycle paths and other facilities is the ideal way to improve cycling safety. But in reality experienced cyclists often avoid using cycle paths, even if this means riding along busy roads.

The value of cycle facilities varies considerably, as does the quality of what is provided. **One of the biggest mistakes a cyclist can make is to think that cycle facilities are inherently safer than using the general roads.** Not all facilities will be safer, particularly for a similar level of mobility, whilst there is evidence that some facilities are both dangerous in themselves and lead to unsafe cycling practices.

Segregation may increase perceived safety compared with riding in traffic, but perceptions of risk – particularly among inexperienced cyclists – are often incorrect. Cycle facilities are usually compromises rather than optimum solutions, for there is rarely the space or money to implement high-quality designs suitable for a broad cross-section of cyclists. Furthermore, some facilities complicate the traffic situation and require cyclists to ride in a way that is not compatible with good cycling practice. Knowledge about cycling is at present very limited amongst facility providers.

Facilities segregated from the carriageway mainly benefit riders who fear motor traffic. As long as they are prepared to ride more slowly and submissively, they can have greater control over (and responsibility for) their own safety. But cyclists who take the trouble to learn the skills of integrating with traffic often find dangers on the road much easier to contend with than the less obvious dangers present on many cycle paths. Using cycle paths can result in these cyclists being more at risk. Furthermore, local knowledge is often essential to the safe use of facilities. In an unfamiliar area, it is usually easier and more predictable to keep with traffic.

To the skilled cyclist, cycle facilities are more likely to offer advantages in terms of convenience rather than safety. You may find them useful where they would result in a shorter, quicker or more agreeable journey. Always be discriminating and cautious, having regard to local circumstances and the purpose of your journey. **Ride within the limits of what you can see to be safe and within your capabilities, never on the assumption that a different route is safer just because it is marked for use by cyclists.** Take advantage of facilities where they help you, but ignore those that don't.

Cycle tracks

Cycle tracks and similar paths away from roads

Ideally, a cycle track should be a carriageway identical in all respects to a road, except for its width and a lack of motor vehicles. In practice, it is rare to find cycle tracks that are as well-designed as roads. Most are the result of compromises in fitting a new track into an existing town infrastructure, whilst some extensive networks built on green-field sites have been designed to very low standards. The result all too often is further hazards with which a cyclist must contend, and frequently an uncomfortable and poorly maintained surface on which to ride.

To use cycle tracks safely requires at least as much skill and concentration as when using the roads, and even the most skilled of cyclists often find themselves having to learn new techniques to deal with the different conditions. Be prepared to ride more slowly than usual, for design speeds of such paths are usually low. Dangers such as bad visibility, sharp bends and steep gradients can be more common on cycle tracks than on the roads, whilst there may also be different hazards to look out for, such as bollards and barriers. Some cycle tracks are more of an obstacle course than a highway! Look out, too, for kerbs at road junctions which have not been laid flush. These can be uncomfortable to cross, and bumping up even a centimetre step too often will damage your bike's headset and affect steering.

Good cycle tracks are clearly signed and marked to indicate road crossings and any other hazards. Don't trust those that aren't, nor ones of unusual design. Take particular care at road junctions, for there is evidence that collisions at these places are on average more serious than ordinary road crashes. If there are barriers or bollards nearby, be careful that manoeuvring past them does not distract your attention from traffic.

The surfaces of cycle tracks are frequently not as comfortable as those of roads, and the lack of regular flexing by wide-tyred vehicles can lead to premature break-up. Setts and blockwork are quite unsuitable for cycling and may be slippery when wet, but both are used on some tracks. Although minor shortcomings might be tolerable on short lengths of track or for low-speed leisure riding, serious defects can pose real problems, whilst, with time or distance, even minor irritations soon accumulate.

Even well-designed cycle tracks are notorious for broken glass, persistent mud and other nuisances, for they do not benefit from the cleansing action of motor vehicles, whose tyres push debris to one side. If you use a poorly surfaced track, keep your weight off the saddle and ride more slowly.

Positioning is as important a consideration on cycle tracks as on roads, but you must allow for the much greater likelihood of oncoming vehicles being on the wrong side – a common cycle track problem. User discipline on cycle tracks is usually much poorer than on roads, even though the consequences of two cyclists, each riding at about 25 km/h (15 mph), colliding head-on are not much different from a single cyclist colliding with a car. The fatalities which have occurred on cycle tracks illustrate this.

The primary riding position should be just to the left of centre of the track, moving well left when meeting someone coming the other way. Take great care at bends, for it is here that most head-on collisions occur. It is not advisable to move too far right for a left-hand bend, as you might on a narrow road, as another cyclist may be cutting the corner. It is easier to see a car coming than a cyclist! Stay left, reduce speed and shout or ring your bell if visibility is bad. Always keep well left on right-hand bends. You will usually have less margin for error on a cycle track than on a road, as there is less distance between vehicles travelling in opposite directions. You must be able to stop within *half* the distance you can see to be clear. It is always safer to give way than to assume that someone else will.

Most cycle tracks are shared with pedestrians, sometimes with segregation – which pedestrians tend not to observe – sometimes not. With similar numbers, cycles and pedestrians generally mix less well than cycles and cars, as discipline is poorer. All walkers are liable to change direction suddenly, but children are particularly unpredictable and need to be passed very cautiously. A ring of a bell, or just a polite 'excuse me' can be useful before overtaking pedestrians. Dogs can be a considerable danger on cycle tracks, where they are more likely to be off the lead than when on a road. Keep well clear.

Roadside cycle tracks

When discussing ways of improving safety for cyclists, many people think intuitively about the provision of cycle tracks adjacent to roads. But these have long been the most controversial of cycling facilities amongst cyclists, rarely used by the great majority of experienced riders. The reasons reflect the often misunderstood differences between perceived and actual danger.

The purpose of a roadside cycle track is to reduce conflict between cyclists and motor traffic by keeping the two apart for as great a distance as possible. However, collisions involving cyclists are not equally likely to happen anywhere along a road. Relatively few occur between junctions, and the one type of collision that roadside tracks reduce, the rear hit, was observed in Chapter 4 to be one of the least common.

Most cyclist crashes occur at junctions and are a result of turning or crossing movements. Roadside cycle tracks usually increase the number of junctions that a cyclist meets, for they are interrupted by every driveway as well as every road. In each case, it is the cyclist who must give way to crossing traffic, unlike on the road, where the cyclist would have the same priority as accompanying vehicles. The result of this is not only a slower and more submissive journey for the cyclist; it also removes much of the burden for taking care from others, and places virtually all the responsibility for avoiding a crash on your shoulders. On the road, not only would you be more likely to receive a clear passage through the junction, but there would be the important safeguard of others being obliged to take care in case you err.

Observing other traffic can be very difficult, too, for it is necessary to look for danger through an angle of up to 270° (Fig. 10.1). This requires much movement of the head, which takes time, and the only way to be really sure that there is no danger from any direction will often be to stop. On the road, you can use positioning and listening to reduce the angle over which you need to concentrate to less than 90° close to a junction, which is within the compass of eye movement alone, and can therefore be carried out much more easily and quickly.

It is particularly difficult from a roadside cycle track to know whether a vehicle on the parallel road will turn into a side road

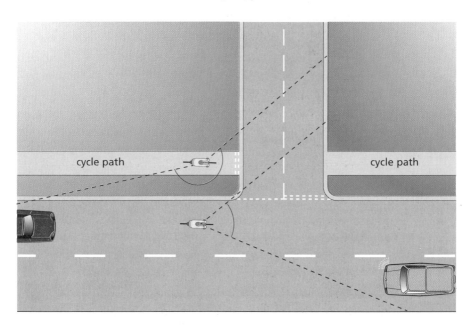

Figure 10.1
Typical surveillance angles from roadside cycle path and road

that you are approaching (you must not rely on signalling by drivers), and you cannot use positioning to deter conflicting movements. This difficulty increases with reduced distance between track and road, or if the road junction design permits fast turning. If in doubt, you must wait.

A further problem of roadside cycle tracks is that they increase the complexity of every junction, for cyclists and motorists alike. For example, a three-way junction becomes a five-way one when a cycle track is added. Making a junction more complicated invariably increases the likelihood of someone making a mistake.

To use roadside cycle tracks safely requires considerable vigilance, and often considerable tolerance too, for such paths are frequently poorly surfaced and get a lot of debris thrown onto them from the road. Footways, re-designated for shared cycle/pedestrian use but without major rebuilding, can be particularly problematic and should be avoided.

The risk of a collision is greatest when using a roadside cycle track in the opposite direction to nearside road traffic flow, because drivers will least expect vehicles to be coming towards them on that side of the road. At night you may be dazzled even by dipped headlights coming towards you.

If you cycle abroad, the use of roadside cycle tracks is often compulsory, although some countries are now reviewing these laws in a bid to cut cycling casualties. Otherwise, nearly the only time when using such a track might be to your advantage is where a well-surfaced track has a long distance between junctions of any kind and the adjacent road is narrow and used by a large number of heavy goods vehicles. This is most likely outside towns, but even here you should recognise that the advantage gained will be mainly one of peace of mind rather than safety, and that you may need to ride more cautiously and submissively than usual.

You should never feel obliged to use a roadside cycle track just because it is there, nor be dissuaded from using a road, if that is your preference, merely because others suggest that you should not.

Cycle lanes

With-flow lanes

With-flow cycle lanes overcome some of the problems of roadside cycle tracks, but they do not improve the safety of cycling. Their greatest benefit is where they result in an increase in the total road space available for manoeuvring. This is most likely where the cycle lane has been added to the width of the adjacent general traffic lane (perhaps by reducing the number of such lanes) rather than being taken from it. Widening the left-hand traffic lane, but without marking a cycle lane, has similar advantages without most of the problems.

The main disadvantage of cycle lanes is that they can effectively restrict the movements of cyclists, encouraging the unsafe practice of riding too far to the left. Some cycle lane markings are placed well to the left of where a cyclist should be riding on an open road, and very few allow for correct positioning when approaching a junction. At the same time, motorists frequently drive up to, if not over, the lane marking and give less clearance to a cyclist than if the lane were not present. The problems are greatest where a lane is narrow, and any lane less than 1.5 metres (5 feet) in width should be treated with great caution.

With all cycle lanes, there can be problems if the lane is obstructed, or where there are pot-holes or debris. When there is no cycle lane, the cyclist has the right of way to pull out in front of following vehicles in order to clear the obstruction. The presence of cycle lane markings removes this priority, creating confusion and requiring you to give way to overtaking traffic.

Where traffic is congested, a with-flow lane may give a cyclist a freer passage, although, as with any other form of filtering, you must watch out for pedestrians crossing and vehicle doors opening. Cycle lanes can, but do not necessarily, lead to a reduction in kerbside parking.

When cycling along a road with a with-flow cycle lane, try not to let it affect your behaviour. In Britain, cyclists are not obliged to keep to a cycle lane, so position yourself as you would if the lane were not there, but be extra careful when moving outside the lane, because other drivers may not expect you to do this. Treat the movement like that of changing lanes on a multi-lane road, moving right by negotiation well in advance of where you need to be in the new position. Be particularly careful to get out of a narrow lane, or to the right side of a wide one, before all junctions, including those with side roads. At principal junctions, join the general traffic lane appropriate to your direction of travel.

Contra-flow lanes

Contra-flow cycle lanes in one-way streets can be useful to cyclists where they enable circuitous detours to be avoided. Like other exemptions, their benefit is mainly one of convenience, except if they enable greater hazards to be by-passed, for contra-flow lanes retain many of the disadvantages of with-flow lanes. Contra-flow bus and cycle lanes are better in as much as they are wider, giving a greater separation from traffic in the opposite direction and allowing you to maintain correct positioning.

Take great care when entering and leaving contra-flow lanes, when passing intermediate junctions and if you need to pass an obstruction by moving outside the lane. Assume that others will not see you. Normally, you should not ride outside the lane because of the danger of conflict with opposing traffic, and special care will be necessary if this requires you to compromise your positioning on the road. Be watchful, too, for the movements of pedestrians. They can easily overlook the presence of a cycle lane while concentrating their attention on traffic from the opposite direction.

Advanced stop lines

At some junctions controlled by traffic signals, advanced stop lines are being introduced to permit cyclists to stop ahead of other traffic. A cycle lane is usually provided at the approach, by which cyclists may filter past waiting vehicles (Figure 10.2). This lane may either be by the kerb or between other traffic lanes.

The benefits of an advanced stop line are that it puts cyclists

Figure 10.2
Advanced stop line
This example is approached by a central cycle lane, which can be useful for
cyclists going ahead when there is a left-turn traffic lane. Other examples are
approached by a kerbside cycle lane.

where they are easily seen by other drivers while waiting for the signals to change to green, and it gives them a head start when the change takes place, allowing the cyclists to clear the junction and build up speed before being passed by other traffic. These are advantages in congested streets and where turning movements are common, especially for slower and less confident riders. There is also the added advantage of not having to wait close to the exhaust pipe of another vehicle.

These advantages during the red phase of the signals must, however, be set against possible dangers at other times. Cyclists who manoeuvre into the reservoir area for cycles as the lights change from red may be vulnerable to other vehicles moving forward. At no time should you cut sharply in front of other traffic. If you are in a cycle lane when the lights change to red-and-amber, negotiate your way back into the traffic stream.

The greatest danger is in attempting to turn right from an advanced stop line approached by a kerbside cycle lane. **Never turn right in traffic directly from the left side of the road.** If you intend to turn right, do not use a kerbside cycle lane, but position normally towards the centre of the road, as if the cycle lane were not there. Move forward to the advanced stop line if it is safe to do so, but otherwise stay with the traffic.

In addition, if you are going straight ahead or left, you shouldn't enter the cycle lane unless there is a clear advantage, bearing in mind the general comments about cycle lanes. When the signals are at green, staying in the general traffic lane may avoid the need to leave and then re-enter the traffic stream, which minimises danger and will probably be quickest, too.

Flank lanes

Sometimes along major roads the white line indicating the edge of the carriageway is some distance from the edge of the road, creating a flank lane. Although not implemented for cyclists – it is intended to minimise road wear by keeping heavy vehicles away from the edge – it may be used as an informal cycle lane.

Flank lanes can be useful in giving a cyclist a little more

clearance from traffic on roads which are typically used by traffic at high speed. Because distances between junctions are usually great, some of the normal disadvantages of cycle lanes are less serious. Much will depend, however, on the lane width, its cleanliness and whether the dividing line includes studs or transverse ridges (to warn drivers going off course), which can be hazardous for a cyclist to cross.

If you use a flank lane, watch out for it ending abruptly, and be sure to leave it at the approach to a junction.

Exemptions

Exemptions for cyclists from banned turns, no-entry restrictions, bus lanes and other controls on general traffic are generally the most useful of all facilities, and were dealt with in Chapter 8. However, even these facilities cannot be considered safe in themselves if a cyclist has to make a movement at variance with other traffic in order to use them, although they can lead to a safer journey overall if they permit greater hazards to be avoided. When using any exemption, always make extra allowance for the fact that others will not expect the movement that you are making.

Cycle routes

In some towns, special routes for cyclists are signed, often using a combination of minor roads and special facilities. Their usefulness to a skilled cyclist is usually low and related to whether or not they permit a quicker journey or allow really difficult junctions to be avoided. Winding or heavily parked routes, those that add significant extra distance or where you frequently have to cede right of way generally have little to recommend them and may actually be less safe than a direct main road. A common disadvantage is the use of local place names on signing, which can make the course of a route unclear to a stranger.

Cycle trails

In many parts of the country, traffic-free cycle trails are being created in order to encourage more people to cycle. These can be very pleasant routes, if not ones generally suited to riding fast, and they are often popular with novices and families.

It is quite wrong, however, to think of these as 'safe' routes, for each year many people are hurt, sometimes very seriously, using cycle trails. The reason is that the paths often demand a degree of skill that is not elementary, yet is rarely appreciated, whilst people think that they are safe and therefore take too little care. Common causes of falls are loose or uneven surfaces, especially on hills, in tunnels and under bridges, and as a result of collisions with other path users and dogs.

To enjoy these trails to the full you need to recognise their limitations, but do not expect others to do likewise!

Many trails have barriers or other physical restrictions which effectively put them out of bounds to tandems, trikes and some other types of cycle.

Road crossings

Various forms of special crossing exist to enable cyclists to cross busy roads independently of other traffic. Sometimes these crossings are linked to cycle tracks on either side; sometimes they are isolated facilities to overcome particular hazards.

Purpose-built cycle underpasses and bridges are theoretically the best and safest forms of crossing. Just how good and safe particular examples are depends very much upon the detailed design and access arrangements, and the general comments about cycle tracks given earlier in the chapter apply. At underpasses it can be useful to use the speed of descent to reduce the effort needed to climb again, but be very careful about this as there are sometimes blind corners and junctions.

Traffic signals are also a satisfactory form of crossing, although they can sometimes result in unnecessary delay to all concerned at less busy times. The usual rules at signals apply.

An unprotected cycle crossing is similar, from a cyclist's point of view, to a conventional crossroads. However, from the point of view of a driver on the road, it must be assumed that it doesn't exist, for it will probably not have the appearance of a conventional junction. The onus, therefore, is always on the cyclist to give way, and to ensure a clear passage before proceeding. The presence of advisory crossing markings does not change this.

Less satisfactory crossings are often found where new facilities have been added to existing road junctions, perhaps by adapting former pedestrian routes. These must be judged on their individual merits, but there's no point in taking a longer or less convenient route if you are able to ride confidently with traffic on the road. Many by-pass facilities are only really suitable for the more timid and slow rider who is prepared to accept the delay and shortcomings of an indirect route. Be particularly cautious about schemes which direct cyclists to use footways in order to avoid a junction, as these frequently introduce more hazards than they remove.

Slip road crossings

These crossings, at split-level junctions on major roads, were dealt with in Chapter 6.

11 — Cycling at night and in all weathers

As an all-purpose means of transport, cycling is not something that stops just because the hour is late or the weather is bad. Cyclists need to travel at all hours of day and night and whatever the weather, but you must modify how you ride to suit the special problems which are met at times when conditions are less favourable.

Cycling at night

This section deals with cycling technique when it is dark. To cycle anywhere at night, good lights are essential, and the requirements for these and other visibility aids are discussed in Chapter 13.

Wherever you ride at night, you must remember that it will be harder for others to see you and it will be harder for everyone – including yourself – to judge conditions. All movements must therefore be made more cautiously, giving time for you to be seen and your intentions understood. Techniques such as negotiation become more difficult when visibility is poor, and it is usually better to use gaps in traffic in order to make complicated manoeuvres. Fortunately, during most hours of darkness, traffic volumes are lower, although this can be offset to some extent by the higher speeds of those drivers who are on the road.

Seeing where you're going is usually only a problem on unlit country roads, where your lights need to be particularly effective. With a powerful beam aimed at the surface about 5–10 metres (about 15–30 feet) ahead, you may be able to proceed at a speed similar to that you could use during the day, but with poorer lights you must be prepared to ride more slowly. The light beam should be angled a little so that you can see the left edge of the road clearly. On a relatively open road this should not be difficult to follow, but where there is dense roadside vegetation, conditions can be very dark and you must look more carefully for where the road goes. The primary riding position will normally keep you away from the worst of the pot-holes and give you warning if you veer off course.

White lines and Cat's-eyes along the road edge or in the centre are a considerable aid to navigation at night, as are reflective road signs giving warning of bends and junctions. Edge markers and reflectors help, too. Signs which may seem superfluous by day take on a new significance when it is dark. The lights of other vehicles can also give useful information about the course that a road takes.

The oncoming headlights of other vehicles, however, can be a considerable hazard to cyclists at night. If blinded, the tendency is to ride straight towards the source of the light, and that could easily be fatal. In any event, dazzle by bright lights will make it harder for you to discern the detail of the road surface ahead of you. Drivers should always dip their lights at the approach of another vehicle, but sometimes low-power cycle lamps are not seen until too late, whilst some drivers mistakenly think that they're helping to light your way by not dipping!

When you meet a vehicle coming in the opposite direction on an unlit road, don't look straight at it. Although you must keep aware of the vehicle's movements, focus your attention on the road ahead, and ensure that you stay a safe distance from the edge. If you are dazzled, slow down, look just ahead of your front wheel and be prepared to stop. Sometimes a flash of your own light by deflecting the handlebars can be successful in reminding a driver to dip. A peaked cap can provide a shield against oncoming headlights and enable you to see the road ahead more clearly.

Cycling at night is certainly more tiring than cycling during the day, as extra concentration is necessary in order to pick out the information you need to plan your movements. In addition, you may already be tired from the activities of the day, whilst in the early hours of the morning the body's metabolism runs slower. Be alert to symptoms of fatigue. If necessary, stop and walk or have a drink (non-alcoholic, and preferably warm) in order to revive yourself.

Wind

Most non-cyclists think that rain is the principal weather problem for cycling. In practice, wind is much worse, although, of course, the combination of wind and rain is worst of all.

The only time when wind is a good thing is when it's behind you, and such occasions seem decidedly rare! Even when it is pushing you along, you need to take care that it doesn't encourage you to go too fast, and that you are not vulnerable to a sidewind or an eddy current as you turn a bend or pass a building or vehicle.

In contrast, headwinds can make cycling a struggle and increase fatigue. The lower and more streamlined your body, the easier it will be to keep going, so if there's no hazard ahead, now is the time to use the drop position if you have dropped handlebars. Change to a lower gear until you can maintain your normal cadence, and try to steer as straight a course as you can.

When riding slowly into a headwind, the secondary riding position will be appropriate away from junctions and will relieve you of the need to give quite so much attention to what's behind. Wind makes it more difficult to hear other traffic. Take care, however, not to drift too close to the road edge, as accurate steering is always more difficult when it's windy. It may be possible to choose a less direct route which avoids the need to ride head-on into the wind for the greater part of the distance.

Crosswinds are the most dangerous type of wind: the full strength of gale force crosswinds can move a cycle sideways across a road. If possible, seek the shelter of roads with hedges, but be careful at gateways and other openings where the wind may suddenly gust against you.

When you must battle against a strong crosswind, keep your body low, engage a low gear and keep firm control of the steering. Most of the time you will need to steer into the wind in order to go straight ahead, but be very cautious about sudden changes in conditions near junctions, buildings and whenever you meet another vehicle.

Rain

As long as you dress appropriately, rain by itself does not have to be unpleasant for cycling. Various types of rainwear are available, and what's best is very much a matter of personal taste. Many cyclists prefer to use a cape because this allows sweat and condensation to escape most easily and it helps to keep the handlebars and gear levers dry. However, a cape can be difficult to control in wind or traffic and can result in less clear hand signals being given, for which a sleeved rainsuit has advantages. Rain hats are available for head protection, but don't use a hood as this may impair visibility. Overshoes can be useful when riding for a long time in the rain.

The primary problem during rain is that your brakes will work less well – possibly much less so. You will need to allow additional time when braking, and to be more cautious approaching possible hazards. Remember to brake with equal force on front and rear brakes.

In heavy rain, it may be some seconds after you pull the levers before the brakes begin to bite, because the blocks must first remove water from the rims. Continue to apply pressure gently; squeezing hard in desperation may result in a wheel locking when rim contact is made, and you may then be thrown off. You should learn how long it takes for your brakes to operate under such conditions.

In very heavy rain you may be quite unable to stop. Of course, you shouldn't get into such a situation in the first place. Chase water off the rims periodically by applying the brakes while riding along. Stop and wait if the rain becomes a deluge, and certainly don't try to descend a steep hill in such conditions.

Rain after a dry spell can result in very slippery roads, as the water mixes with surface oil. Take particular care at bends and near junctions.

Spray from overtaking traffic can be a problem, both during rain and for some time after; heavy lorries are a particular nuisance in this respect. If you can, try to pace your riding so that you are not overtaken near large puddles on the road, possibly by adopting the primary riding position at such places. In any event, take care that puddles are not pot-holes in disguise; if in doubt, keep clear.

You should bear in mind that although your visibility will not be greatly impaired by rain (unless you wear spectacles), that of motorists may be. In the winter, windscreens often steam up, especially if a vehicle heater is in use. This can considerably reduce a driver's ability to see you, and is another reason for riding with special caution during wet weather.

Thunderstorms

You either like thunder and lightning or you don't, but thunderstorms present two special problems for cyclists. The first is that the rain is likely to be heavy, and all the previous comments about braking in heavy rain apply. Secondly, in exposed areas there is a small, but real, risk of a cyclist being hit by lightning. This is most likely if you are one of the tallest objects around, as might be the case on an open moor. Under such circumstances you should try to seek cover (but not under a tree!) until the storm passes.

Snow, ice and cold weather

It may not be the most pleasant time for cycling when the temperature is below freezing point and the roads are covered by snow or ice, but cycling is nevertheless possible in all but the most severe of conditions.

The first requirement is to wrap up well. Warm hands are essential for proper braking, but take care that gloves or mittens do not impede the use of the brake levers. Sheepskin gloves are amongst the warmest. A woolly hat or balaclava will restrict heat loss from the head; it should certainly cover the ears, which feel the cold a lot when cycling. Warm socks and shoes are also important; despite the pedalling, toes remain relatively motionless, and in a cold draught can become numb very quickly. If you're going a long way, take a flask with a hot drink, and some additional clothes.

From November until at least the end of March, always assume there will be ice after a cold night, and start out cautiously. Even if all seems clear, there may still be ice hollows where the road dips or turns, or at other places for no apparent reason. Reducing tyre pressure just a little can give better adhesion on slippery surfaces, and is worth doing if there is a lot of snow or ice. Winter is definitely not the time to use treadless tyres.

Make every move gently – starting, cornering and braking. Be as relaxed as possible, but always ready for a tumble. Brake as little as possible, and only when steering straight. Ride slowly, in a lower gear than normal, and regulate your speed as far as possible by changing your cadence. It is important to keep both hands on the handlebars as much as you can. As long as you do not pedal too hard, you are more stable pedalling than freewheeling. Where there's a risk of falling, select a low gear and pedal gently all the time, and against the brakes downhill. Never make sharp turns; if necessary, stop to check that all is clear, change direction and then ride off again in a straight line. Don't be rushed by traffic or allow yourself to be pushed into the roadside slush, but do try to keep out of others' way where possible.

If you see ice ahead that you can't avoid, keep going in a straight line. As long as you stay relaxed and do not turn, the chances of toppling are not very great. Skidding can be caused by braking, accelerating or changing direction. If your rear wheel skids, this can often be corrected by easing off power and freewheeling a little, steering straight. Front wheel skids are very difficult to correct, but if you have the presence of mind, try to restore your body and the cycle to an upright position and you may succeed. Alternatively, you may be able to put a foot down quickly to counter a skid.

Fresh, uncompacted snow is usually easy to cycle through as long as it is not too deep, and after recent snowfall it can be best to keep to those parts of a road not yet travelled by other vehicles. On the other hand, the ridges of ice produced by the thawing and re-freezing of snow probably present the most dangerous conditions for cycling. When in doubt, get off and walk.

Snowfall itself makes cycling difficult, even if it does not settle. Snow flakes can badly sting the eyes, making it hard to look ahead. Spectacles or other forms of eye protection do not really help, for they are easily obscured by falling flakes. A peaked cap is probably the best solution. At night, snowfall can be hypnotic, distracting attention from the road.

Fog and mist

At times of bad visibility a cyclist is particularly vulnerable. Use your lights as if it were night-time, but allow for the fact that the light from your lamps will penetrate much less far. Keep closer to the road edge than usual, both to allow for the fact that others will have greater difficulty seeing you and so that you can follow the road more easily. In dense fog, keep your speed well down, otherwise you will have less warning than you need of pot-holes and the like. Do not follow another vehicle too closely: it may have to stop suddenly. Fog and mist can seriously impair braking, in a similar way to rain, and you should allow for this.

When seeing is difficult, hearing becomes an even more important sense for the cyclist. Listen carefully for the movements of others. In this way you can change, if you wish, between the position and speed best suited to your progress and those best suited to your protection. Don't hesitate to shout if it might help someone detect your presence.

Fog, mist, fine rain and perspiration transfer salt from the face into your eyes, which can lead to eye irritation and fatigue. In these conditions use a cloth or a glove to wipe at least your forehead from time to time.

Sun

The brightness of a sunny day can be very tiring for a cyclist, and sunglasses and a hat are useful accessories. Polarising sunglasses are particularly useful in reducing the glare reflected by road surfaces. Another hazard to heed is the hypnotic effect of a low sun to your side, broken up by a series of closely spaced trees or railings which result in pulses of bright light across your path. Slow down if you experience this, and look low.

In hot climates, sunstroke or sunburn are the main problems of which to be wary, and can be encountered in Britain more regularly than many people imagine. Dehydration is also a hazard which can occur anywhere: always carry something to drink when cycling in hot weather.

Another very distinct danger is that either you or another driver may be temporarily blinded. This is most likely to occur when a bright sun is low in the sky and within the field of view of a driver looking ahead. It can happen in the centre of a town as easily as in the middle of the countryside. If you are riding in line with the direction of the sun, make extra allowance for the fact that any driver heading towards it may be blinded and fail to see you. If you are blinded yourself, concentrate on the road immediately ahead, and slow down.

12 — Tandems, tricycles and recumbents

Tandems

Cycling can give enormous pleasure on any kind of machine, but for most people who try it, riding a tandem is the ultimate cycling experience. The two riders share every aspect of their journey, acting as a team, helping each other along and enjoying the ability to converse socially with ease as they go. Tandeming is more than twice the fun of riding a solo cycle.

A tandem is a remarkably effective machine at promoting equity. Strong and weak riders can ride together at all times, each contributing to the effort required as they are able. Riding a tandem can also bring the joy of cycling to people who could never cycle alone. Blind and partially-sighted people can ride as 'stokers' – playing as full a part in propelling the machine as a person with normal sight – as can people who find it difficult to balance on their own. Young children can also be tandem partners, contributing their effort to covering quite substantial distances without having to cope by themselves with difficult traffic conditions.

Riding together

Tandem partners need to perform as one, so it is essential for there to be an excellent personal relationship between them. The 'pilot' is 'in charge', and the 'stoker' needs to respond promptly to changes in pedalling demand and to requests for signals and reports on the traffic situation. At the same time the stoker must have complete confidence in the pilot with regard to all decisions made in traffic. Unlike a passenger in a car, the stoker has direct influence on the motion of the vehicle, but must cede to the pilot the principal decisions as to when to exert that influence.

Although most people are able to enjoy tandeming after only a little practice, there are, alas, some people for whom the psychological demands are just too great.

The roles of pilot and stoker

The pilot – also known sometimes as the 'helmsman' or 'captain' – is responsible for steering, braking, changing gear and manoeuvring on the road. The stoker, who is at the back (except on some recumbent tandems), co-operates in supplying pedalling effort as required and usually undertakes signalling and map-reading. The stoker may also operate an auxiliary brake on steep descents.

To a large extent, the demands on the pilot are the same as those when riding a solo bicycle. Indeed, it is possible for a pilot to ride a tandem solo, when it is usual to use bungee cords to connect together the front and rear pedals so that toe clips do not drag along the ground on corners. When the pilot decides to pedal, he or she does so; when the pilot wants to stop pedalling, he or she stops. The pilot controls the tandem in almost all the ways that are necessary in order to match the requirements of traffic, terrain and direction.

The stoker soon learns to follow the pedalling actions of the pilot, which are transmitted directly through the linking chain, and to continue pedalling for as long as the pedals are turning. The pilot must take care not to spin the pedals too quickly, or the stoker's feet may be thrown off.

Where traffic conditions do not dictate the riding style, each rider needs to be sensitive to the other rider's wishes to vary pace or to freewheel from time to time. The stronger rider of a pair should take special care not to force the pace.

When changing gear, the stoker should learn to detect automatically the slight relaxation in pressure on the chain in order to allow a smooth transition, and to follow suit. Until this skill is perfected, it is helpful for the pilot to warn his or her partner that a gear change is about to take place.

Verbal communication between pilot and stoker is important to respond properly to traffic conditions. If rapid acceleration is required, the stoker must be asked to assist, whilst the stoker has an important job keeping track of the movements of following vehicles – perhaps as a prerequisite to turning – and reporting this to the pilot. Although the pilot retains overall responsibility for the tandem, with a good stoker to assist, manoeuvring in traffic can be easier than when riding solo. Also, other road users generally show more courtesy to tandems, in part because they are uncommon and often provide a conversation point.

The pilot should give a verbal warning to his or her partner when approaching bumps and dips in the road (including speed humps) and other surface irregularities. In response, the stoker should hold on firmly and lift his or her weight off the saddle to ensure a safer and more comfortable ride for everyone.

Giving responsibility for signalling to the stoker (this cannot be done with young children) is particularly useful in assisting progress through traffic. A stoker may signal continuously, irrespective of traffic conditions, and engage eye-to-eye contact with following drivers in a way that is not otherwise possible. Although the act of signalling is usually carried out by the stoker, this is done in response to requests from the pilot, who should warn the stoker as early as possible of manoeuvres. The stoker must be ready to respond to requests immediately.

Because of their weight, tandems should be equipped with a third brake, usually in the form of a hub or disc brake acting on the rear wheel. It can be useful to give control of this brake to the stoker, both in order to spread the hand effort required to apply the brakes, and to have an emergency brake under independent control should a main brake fail. It is essential, however, that the stoker is disciplined about the use of the extra brake, which must only be applied in response to a request by the pilot. If the stoker were to apply the brake at a time when the pilot had decided to accelerate to avoid a conflict, the consequences could be serious. It is imperative that all decisions about the motion of a tandem rest with the pilot.

An auxiliary role for the stoker which has many benefits is as navigator and map-reader. On a solo bicycle it is hazardous to read a map while going along, but the stoker on a tandem can do this easily. The stoker should practise riding with no hands on the handlebars (toe clips are essential), which enables a map to be held and unfolded as required. However, the stoker should grasp the handlebars at the approach of any hazard.

Gaining proficiency

In some ways, when you first ride a tandem it is like learning to cycle all over again, especially if neither pilot nor stoker have ridden such a machine before. Although you will soon get used to it, an important difference between riding a solo and a tandem is that in the former you compensate only for your own movements, whilst on a tandem you must adjust to the movements of your partner as well, and these are less predictable. It is not unusual on a first tandem ride to wobble from side to side in quite an unnerving manner, and practice will be necessary for you both to learn the new balancing skills. Keep relaxed and use a low gear.

There are two alternative ways to move off on a tandem. In the first option, the stoker is seated and puts both feet into the toe clips while the pilot, astride the crossbar, holds the tandem steady. When the stoker is settled, the pilot pushes off in a similar manner as to start a solo bicycle, and the stoker adds power to achieve speed and balance. This is usually the best – and may be the only – option when the stoker is much shorter or lighter than the pilot, or with a child stoker using kiddy cranks (see Figure 12.1). The stoker must have confidence in the pilot's ability to hold the tandem steady, and the pilot must fulfil that confidence.

The other way to start a tandem is for both riders to push off as if they are on separate solos. Each rider, seated, puts one foot in its toe clip and then they push off together with the other foot. This method requires greater synchronisation and is best suited to partners of similar weight and build, but it can result in quicker starts, which are an advantage in traffic.

Differences in riding technique

Whilst most of the skills acquired for a solo cycle apply equally to a tandem, there are some differences in technique because a tandem is heavier and longer.

One is that a tandem is slower and more sluggish to accelerate than a solo. This is felt particularly in town traffic, where a tandem is less able to get away quickly from traffic signals and other stops. This will have consequences for your ability to keep up with traffic, and you may find that progress is therefore slower.

Similarly, tandems stop more slowly than solos when the brakes are applied, and more hand pressure is required on the brake levers for a given stopping distance. This is also a particular disadvantage in towns, when the stop-go nature of traffic can be very wearing for both a tandem and its riders. Tandems are not well suited to circumstances where car drivers overtake fast and then hit the brakes sharply to stop.

It is important to agree the technique to be used when a stop and restart are necessary, such as at junctions. The pilot alone or both riders may put a foot down when stopping. The pilot will then reposition the pedals for restarting, and the stoker should accommodate this. A quick word from the pilot is useful as the tandem moves off to confirm to the stoker that now is the time to add power.

Where riders are well matched, hill climbing on a tandem is only marginally more difficult than on solos, but with the more usual combination of unmatched riders, climbing hills is more strenuous. It is more important than ever to change down in gear in good time and for both riders to develop a smooth rhythm to their pedalling. Aligning the cranks of one rider at 90° to those of the other can result in a more efficient pedalling technique, but this practice can make synchronisation difficult at other times and is probably of little overall benefit.

Going downhill, a tandem can travel significantly faster than a solo, although whether or not it is wise to take advantage of this will depend upon the circumstances. The benefits of a third brake on a tandem have already been mentioned for use on steep or long descents. If this brake is applied through a ratchet-operated gear-type lever (often inset into one end of the handlebars), efficient braking can be achieved without continuous hand pressure. However, hub and disc brakes are not suitable for rapid deceleration, so do make sure that your speed never exceeds that from which you can stop within the distance you can see to be clear.

A considerable benefit of tandems is the fact that the vehicle has twice the pedal-power for only one-and-a-half times the wind resistance of a solo bicycle. This means that progress against a strong headwind is much easier, the stoker in particular being less affected by it. Sidewinds, too, are less troublesome as its additional weight makes a tandem more stable.

Riding with a visually-impaired stoker

Tandeming with a blind or visually-impaired stoker can be an enjoyable experience for both partners, and most of the general advice on riding a tandem applies. The main difference between riding with a visually-impaired rather than a sighted stoker is that the stoker is less able to predict changes of circumstances. The pilot must therefore give attention to keeping the stoker fully informed of events that might affect progress while riding. Frequent oral communication is very important.

A good cyclist will always try to anticipate road conditions to avoid sudden movements, whether on account of traffic or surface hazards. With a blind stoker this is all the more important, to ensure that the stoker is not taken by surprise. Try not to stop suddenly, in case the stoker is thrown forward in a frightening way. Always give a succinct explanation if unusual movements are required.

At junctions, describe the traffic situation and road layout to your partner, and express aloud your thought process in deciding how best to manoeuvre.

Always forewarn the stoker of approaching hills, whether they are going up or down, the approximate length and severity. Some tandemists use a scale of 1 to 10 to assess gradient in a way that enables the stoker to make meaningful comparisons.

Give warning of bends, so that the stoker will not be worried when the tandem starts to lean. The stoker should be told in advance whether the bend is to left or right and how severe it is likely to be. It is also important to announce when the bend actually begins. Similarly, when turning at road junctions, give both advance warning and a further warning as you start to turn. The stoker may do the signalling, but will need to be told when to stop as well as when to start.

You should also learn the other situations that can cause discomfort that is unpredictable to someone who cannot see. For example, when you enter a wood there can be a sudden change of temperature. A long bridge or tunnel over the road brings a change in the ambient sound. By describing the surroundings at regular intervals you keep the stoker aware, as well as adding interest to the journey.

Communication with a blind stoker is not a one-way process. Visually-impaired people often have a more acute sense of hearing than a sighted person, and you should take advantage of this to detect traffic movements and other hazards earlier.

Finally, don't forget your partner when you reach your destination! You will need to be extra careful getting on and off the tandem in order not to strike the stoker, who may also need to be escorted from the bike to a place of safety.

Tandems with children

Tandems afford families with young children the ability to cover significant distances by cycle, whilst the children themselves enjoy the experience of riding a 'full-size' bike at such an early age.

The simplest way to enable young children to ride tandem is by fitting 'kiddy cranks' – a separate bottom bracket, chainset and pedals fitted to the rear down tube at a height which the child, sitting on the rear saddle, can reach (Figure 12.1). The normal rear cranks are removed and the link chain re-routed to the kiddy cranks' chainwheel. It is also necessary to extend the rear handlebars so that they can be reached easily by the child. Kiddy cranks can be used by children from about the age of four, as

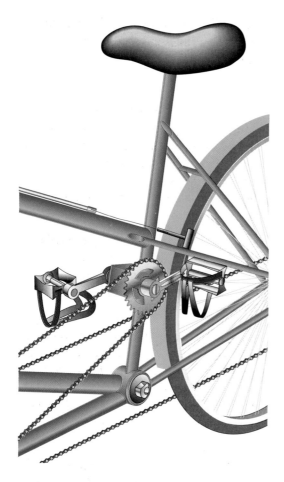

Figure 12.1
Kiddy cranks

soon as they have the ability to remain seated still. The use of toe clips is important so that the child's feet do not slip, and is all that is usually required to keep the child secure.

Cycling with a child on a tandem becomes progressively harder work for the pilot until such time as the child is able to contribute meaningfully to the pedalling (around 9 years), and control of the machine is also more difficult. This needs to be taken into account when manoeuvring in traffic. None the less, young children can contribute usefully to the power required over relatively short distances, such as when climbing hills, and this should be encouraged. The rest of the time the child's legs will spin as the pilot pedals. Using kiddy cranks, the child's legs will rotate much faster than the pilot's, but the child soon becomes used to this and there are no untoward consequences.

Although responsibility for signalling should not be given to young children and the pilot should always ensure that clear hand signals are given, it is good to teach children to signal as soon as possible. This has the advantage of developing good signalling technique, which will then be copied when the child rides his or her own bike. Tandeming is in general a good way for children to acquire traffic skills.

Tricycles

Tricycles have distinct qualities as a form of human-powered vehicle that gain them many advocates. But they are more than just enthusiast machines, for they have unique advantages which can benefit a wider public. This section concentrates on the more usual type of tricycle with one wheel at the front and two behind. There are also models with the two wheels at the front, and recumbent variants of each.

The stability of a tricycle is a great asset. On icy roads a trike may skid, but it is very unlikely to fall over. In high winds, a trike is less susceptible to being blown across the road than a two-wheeler. People who find it difficult to balance on a bicycle are often able to ride a trike.

A tricycle handles very well when heavily loaded: an advantage when shopping or for taking camping gear on holiday. The same applies for carrying children – a solo trike can be fitted with one or two child seats, or a tandem trike can have a child stoker. It is simple for a parent to lift a child on and off a trike, as there is no need to hold the trike upright.

In towns, tricycles are less manoeuvrable in congested streets and are often forced to follow the queue of traffic. Some cycle facilities are also too narrow to be used with ease. On the other hand, a tricyclist can gain a good view over cars by sitting up in the saddle, and where changes of direction are required, a trike can turn around almost on the spot. It is also easy to restart a tricycle in traffic, for there is no initial wobble.

One great convenience of a trike is that it can be parked anywhere, as support is not required. However, a parking brake is essential if the vehicle is not to go for a ride on its own!

Learning to ride a tricycle

If you have never ridden a bicycle, then riding a trike is easy. Just get on and go! It is rather more difficult for a bicyclist to adapt to a tricycle. The reason has more to do with the peculiarities of bicycle riding than with anything special about a tricycle.

Riding a bicycle is a balancing act. The machine is inherently unstable, and subtle movements of the body counteract the bicycle's tendency to fall first in one direction and then the other. A tricycle, on the other hand, is perfectly stable. It is not necessary to compensate for oscillations from side to side, as there are none. Yet a bicycle rider will intuitively seek to do this.

The difference in riding technique is most noticeable when turning a bend. As was pointed out in Chapter 2, a bicycle is rarely steered around a bend, but moves in the required direction by the bicyclist leaning slightly into the curve. Leaning will not make a tricycle turn, however – it needs to be steered! A bicyclist riding a trike must therefore learn to steer when turning.

Find a large, flat area, such as an empty car park, for some practice. Pedal slowly – very low speeds and stopping are no problem on a trike – and apply the brakes if the machine does not go where you want it to. Then try again. Closing your eyes can help to counter your instinctive bicycling balance. With a little practice you will soon succeed.

Although leaning on a trike will not initiate a turn, leaning is none the less necessary in addition to steering when cornering sharply or at speed in order to keep both rear wheels on the ground. If there is not enough lean, the wheel on the inside of the turn will lift up. You therefore lean in the direction to which you wish to turn. The amount of lean required is more pronounced than when riding a bicycle, and to facilitate this be sure to push the pedal down on the side to which you lean. Do not try cornering fast until you have perfected this technique.

Tricycles with a rigid rear axle are the most difficult to handle on corners due to drag, whilst machines with single-wheel drive suffer from slippage. Two-wheel drive, through coupled freewheels or a differential transmission system, is an asset.

Tricycles are much more affected by the camber of the road than are bicycles, and this has a marked effect on steering. When the camber slopes down to the left it is necessary to steer right to compensate, and vice versa. Some British tricycles are built with the rear axle offset slightly about the line of the front wheel in order to assist handling on typical cambers. However, such machines are all the more difficult to ride in countries that drive on the right!

A tricycle is a three-track vehicle – each wheel follows its own path – compared with the single track of a bicycle, where one wheel generally follows the other. This means that tricyclists need to be much more adept at avoiding pot-holes and other bad surfaces. Although a trike is less likely to be overturned, pot-holes can still damage wheels and cause discomfort.

A tricycle has more drag than a bicycle on account of the extra wheel and long axle. This can make hill climbing more strenuous. On the other hand, you can use very low gears more easily as effort is not wasted in maintaining balance, and you can also stop to have a rest and then restart with comparative ease.

On many trikes, both brakes act on the front wheel (because it is difficult to fit brakes to the rear wheels), and on these machines in particular, going downhill requires care. It has already been mentioned that cornering at speed requires special skill, and in general, tricycles are less well suited to fast descents than bicycles. Care is always needed when braking on a curve, as this has a marked effect on the handling of the tricycle.

Recumbent cycles

The differences between conventional cycles are to a large degree due to subtle changes of geometry, gearing and wheels. Recumbents, on the other hand, come in a much wider range of shapes and sizes, and have greatly increased the variety of cycles to choose from. Recumbent tandems and tricycles are available, as well as recumbent solo bicycles.

Common advantages of recumbent cycles are greater efficiency and comfort. Recumbent cycling means an end to saddle-soreness, neck ache and pressure on the hands; some people with back problems especially can benefit.

From a safety point of view, weight is more evenly distributed on a recumbent, and this means that more braking force can be obtained from the front brake until ultimately the front wheel skids. It is almost impossible to be pitched over the front wheel, whilst in a frontal impact it is the rider's feet which make contact first, rather than the upper body. A frequent concern about recumbents is that in some (but by no means all) models the rider is lower than on a sports cycle, and recumbents can be difficult to see over a car. This is probably more of a perceived problem than a real one, for recumbents certainly attract a lot of attention. If necessary, an upright flag on a lightweight pole can be added. Recumbents with colourful fairings are often imposing vehicles which make it easy to command a place on the road.

Riding a recumbent

Long-wheelbase recumbents are the easiest for newcomers to get on and ride confidently. They are very stable and usually have the pedals close to the ground, making it easy to put a foot down when stopping. Being relaxed is the main requirement to ride one of these machines successfully.

Short-wheelbase recumbents are lighter and more manoeuvrable than their longer cousins, with a more laid-back riding position. One consequence of this is that the pedals are much higher off the ground, and more practice is needed to gain confidence. Although good for achieving speed, it is more difficult to make tight low-speed manoeuvres.

Handlebars on a recumbent may be either above or below the legs. The low bar position is not the optimum aerodynamically, but otherwise affords very relaxed control of the bike, requiring only a light touch. Compared with a conventional bicycle, it is less easy to move your body weight when turning, and more movement of the handlebars is required.

It is also less easy to benefit from ankling when pedalling a recumbent, and more power comes from a straight push. On the other hand, the stiff seat helps good acceleration to be achieved, which adds to the recumbent's significant aerodynamic advantage. Climbing hills may mean using a lower gear, as force from the upper body cannot assist in pedalling.

Forward visibility from a recumbent is excellent, but side views over hedges tend to be lost. It is also more difficult to turn your body to see behind, so a rear view mirror can be useful. Emerging from side roads, too, is less easy than on a conventional cycle, as the rider is further back and can see less of the crossing road. These situations require you to act as if you are in a car, stopping at the junction and leaning forward to obtain the best view. In general, recumbents are not best suited for riding in heavy traffic.

Most recumbents have the rider's arm height below that of car roofs. This means that hand signals need some care. Always keep sufficiently far from other vehicles that clear signals may be given, retracting your arm briefly if someone drives too close.

Other occasions which require special care are when meeting animals. The coloured fairings of some recumbents can be more frightening to a horse than a conventional cycle, and if a dog attacks, the cyclist is within easier reach.

13 — Safety and riding aids

In recent years, much equipment has appeared on the market which claims to improve the safety of cyclists. There is little evidence that the majority of these items make any significant contribution towards cycling safety, whilst some produce secondary hazards which can negate any usefulness. Scepticism should therefore always be the first reaction to claims of this kind.

There is another problem with safety aids – the human factor. There is evidence that as people become better protected – or think that they are – they take more chances, until their overall risk level is much as before. If safety aids make you feel safer, it is likely that you will ride less carefully or more adventurously, and you may end up being no safer than previously. It is important to realise that much of the decision to act more riskily is subconscious; you therefore need to take positive steps to counter it.

No safety aid will adequately compensate for a poor riding style, and no aid is anything like as effective in reducing the likelihood of a cyclist being injured as learning to control a cycle properly in the first place. Conversely, you will probably find that, having learnt to ride skillfully, many aids are of very limited value.

This chapter assesses the usefulness of a variety of supposed safety aids, but first looks at a number of items of more conventional equipment which, though seldom promoted for the purpose, have proven to enhance the safety and efficiency of cycling.

Alloy rims and better brakes

The two greatest deficiencies of a cycle compared with motor vehicles are limited acceleration and poor braking. There isn't a lot that can be done to a cycle to significantly increase acceleration (lightweight and aerodynamically shaped components help, but only to a degree useful to the racing devotee), but there are ways of improving the braking of the average machine. Probably the most important single 'safety aid' for a cyclist is to use wheels with alloy rims rather than steel ones, for the improvement in braking performance is marked, especially in the wet. Although it is possible to improve braking with steel rims by the use of leather-faced brake blocks, their all-weather performance still cannot match that of good blocks acting on alloy rims.

A number of advances have been made in brake block materials, and hard compounds are now available which have considerably better stopping power than before. There are penalties for this, though: it can be easier to lock a wheel when braking hard, whilst some blocks have such a high-friction surface that they noticeably accelerate rim wear.

Most modern brake mechanisms work well, but if you want to achieve the best braking possible, then cantilever brakes are the most efficient in terms of the hand effort necessary to achieve a certain braking force. Many all-terrain and hybrid bikes are fitted with cantilever brakes, but otherwise these are rare. As they must be fitted to bosses brazed onto the cycle frame and forks, they can only be added when having a new frame built, or an old one renovated.

Brake lever extensions are available for hybrid bikes which enable the brakes to be applied more easily from the alternative handlebar holding positions.

Extension levers are also available for dropped handlebars, but these are only suitable for use on long, gradual descents, where the road ahead is clear, for they cannot bring a cycle to a halt quickly. Never use them in traffic, in the likely presence of other hazards, or if a hill is steep.

Toe clips and clipless pedals

Often thought by the inexperienced to be a safety hazard, toe clips – used with the straps loose – can be a great safety asset once you have mastered using them. When riding in stop-go traffic they prevent shoes slipping from the pedals and enable quick restarting. They also greatly improve the efficiency of pedalling. If you haven't used toe clips before, try just the right one first, and always keep the straps loose. Half-clips are also available that do not use straps at all.

To use toe clips, engage one foot in its clip before you start off. The other clip will naturally hang downwards, which means that it will not interfere with you using the back of the second pedal for pedalling during the first few metres if you need to. As soon as you can, pause pedalling and knock the rear of the second pedal downwards with your toe, moving your foot backwards and out of the way at the same time. The toe clip will rotate to the top, when you should move your foot quickly forwards and into the clip. With practice you should be able to engage the second toe clip within half a revolution of the pedals after starting.

To remove a foot from its toe clip, just pull it back. As long as you keep the straps loose, you should not find that using toe clips interferes with putting a foot down when stopping.

Clipless pedals are a development from toe clips, and are used in conjunction with special shoes or shoe plates. The shoes clip directly into the pedal by stepping onto it. To release your foot, just twist and pull. The release tension can be adjusted, and you should start with this at minimum. It is also a good idea to use two-sided or flat pedals so that you can use either side when you start off.

Recumbent cyclists find clipless pedals especially useful, as there is a tendency for feet to slip out of toe clips.

Bells, horns and sirens

The only situation in which the traditional bicycle bell is useful is when using paths shared with pedestrians. In quiet surroundings it can be a unobtrusive way of letting non-motorised travellers know you're there. In virtually all instances, however, it is equally effective, and more acceptable, to slow down and say a polite 'Excuse me.'

In traffic, a bell is useless and more of a safety liability than an aid. Shouting can be effective, but on most occasions it is far better for cyclists to give all their attention to taking evasive action if another vehicle or pedestrian is heading their way.

Horns have no purpose. On paths their sound is too abrupt, and as likely to frighten someone into your way as out of it, and in traffic they are as ineffective as bells.

Aerosol-operated sirens are available for cycles, and the louder ones can be heard inside cars. Their sound is more offensive than a verbal warning, and in most instances a cyclist should be busy avoiding a potential collision rather than sounding off about it.

Conspicuity and perspicuity

It is important to safety on the road that your presence is noticed by others. But that is not sufficient, for the way in which other road users react to you will depend not only upon the fact that they have seen you, but also upon who or what they perceive you to be, and on how far away they think you are. For instance, a driver who mistakes your rear reflector for a reflective road edge marker may fail to pull out to pass you. Nor will a driver manoeuvre so early if you appear to be further ahead than you are.

To be really safe on the road, therefore, you must not only be seen, but you must be seen to be a *cyclist*, and your position must be judged accurately. Perspicuity – being clearly understood – is more important than simple conspicuity, and this is particularly so if you are riding along a road where cyclists are few and far between.

Unfortunately, many of the so-called visibility aids available for cyclists attempt only to achieve conspicuity, whilst some can actually convey misleading information about the other details which are so important to pin-pointing a cyclist on the road. Before using any aid intended to make your presence more obvious, you should always consider just how well it portrays the complete picture.

Be careful, too, not to cause visual confusion by the use of too many different devices; the 'decorated Christmas tree' approach advocated by some has little merit. Good perspicuity requires conveying simple, easy-to-decipher information about your presence; overdoing it may prove counter-productive.

Lights

Good lights are essential for cycling at night, as well as being a legal requirement. In comparison with good, bright lights, no other visibility aid is anything like as easy for other road users to see. A single white light at the front and a single red light at the rear makes a cyclist clearly conspicuous, and strongly suggests a two-wheeled vehicle. The relatively slow speed of a cyclist and the natural wobble would probably suggest to an observant driver that the vehicle is in fact a cycle and enable a good estimate of position, but lamps alone do not make a cyclist perspicuous at night.

The best lamps use rechargeable batteries and halogen bulbs, but are relatively expensive. Care needs to be taken to re-charge the batteries frequently and before any long trip. Dynamo lights are usually reliable in dry weather, but much less so in the wet. The variation of lighting level with speed, with no light if you stop, can be a hazard, although there are some back-up systems available which switch to a standby battery as you slow down. Ordinary battery lamps have improved in recent years, but the batteries need changing after only a few hours' use if the light emitted is to remain sufficient. Always carry spare batteries, and whatever type of lights you use, carry spare bulbs of the correct type.

Make sure that lamps are securely fixed to the cycle, either along its centre line or to the offside. They should point directly forward and back. A front lamp lights the road ahead better if mounted on the front fork or a front carrier than on the headset, but only do this if there is a lamp boss fitted. Direct the beam to fall on the road 5–10 metres (about 15–30 feet) ahead.

Some cyclists use more than one lamp at front or rear to boost their lighting. This is not such a good idea as first it seems, since drivers may perceive the two lamps a short distance apart as those of a car much further away, and not realise that it is a cycle until too close to avoid a collision. With good lamps, more than one light at front or rear is unnecessary and unlikely to achieve any practical advantage.

Some lights on sale use light-emitting diodes (LEDs). Although these have much potential for the development of efficient cycle lighting with long battery life, many of those at present available have a total light output which is much lower than that of conventional filament-bulb lamps. In particular, LEDs can have a very restricted angle of light emission and be much less visible off axis. A wide dispersion characteristic is important for cycle lights. Some LED lamps can be set to flash intermittently. This further reduces the light output, relying upon the relative novelty of the effect to gain attention. It is illegal to fit flashing lights to a cycle.

Reflectors

A red rear reflector is a legal requirement at night, but in the presence of good lights it adds little extra information about a cycle or its progress. The main value of such a reflector probably lies in the modest amount of protection it affords cyclists who persist in riding without lights.

The front and spoke reflectors fitted to new cycles are in much the same category, although there is no legal obligation to use them. Front reflectors are only fully effective if oncoming drivers do not dip their lights, which is a considerable hazard to a cyclist and should not be encouraged. Spoke reflectors are of very limited value. The movement of the reflectors will only convey their message to a driver who is some way off along a side road, and who is thus unlikely to be involved in a collision; they are unlikely to be seen in time from a vehicle closer by.

The only type of reflector that adds significantly to perspicuity in the presence of good lights is that which can be fitted to the pedals. When fitted, the up and down movement of the pedals is easily picked up by a headlamp beam, and the movement is unique to a pedal cyclist. The amount of up and down movement also conveys useful information as to how far away the cyclist is. Pedal reflectors are one of the most effective safety aids for cyclists at night, but they need to be kept clean and in good repair in order to retain their advantages.

Clothing

It is sensible for cyclists to wear light-coloured clothing at any time, but it is unproven that additional visibility aids have much advantage during the day. It is likely that the way cyclists ride, and in particular the position taken on the road, has much more effect on how easily others see and react to them. Special high-visibility jackets are available and have been shown to reduce the number of close passes by drivers overtaking a cyclist. However, brightly coloured ordinary clothes are almost as effective, much cheaper, and less obtrusive off the bike.

Reflective belts and sashes aid perspicuity, although only in a similar way to lights, for they do not clearly differentiate a cyclist from a motorcyclist or moped rider. They are most effective on dark country roads, especially around dawn and dusk, but much less so during the day or under street lights. They are particularly useful if you need to wear dark clothing for some reason when you cycle. One unfortunate side effect of the devices, however, can be that oncoming drivers are more reluctant to dip their headlights, for this reduces the intensity of the reflected image they receive back.

Reflective bands are available for arms and legs, and strips can be bought for the cycle and luggage. Fluorescent garments are also available, but these are of no use at night.

Helmets

Cycle helmets differ from other safety aids in that they attempt only to limit the consequences of a crash. They do nothing to prevent a crash taking place; indeed, if not used properly or if their limitations are not appreciated, they may actually increase that risk.

Helmet wearing by cyclists is a controversial and often emotional subject. It is important to keep the risk of head injury in perspective. Head injury when cycling is neither inevitable nor common, especially for people who learn to ride skillfully.

A helmet works through absorbing some of the force of an impact by itself deforming. The core of shock-absorbing material acts as a buffer which reduces the acceleration forces that reach the head. In this way a helmet can provide an additional margin against injury, particularly following a simple fall or a glancing, low-speed collision.

However, the protection afforded by a cycle helmet is quite limited. Over half of head injuries to cyclists affect parts of the head for which a helmet offers no protection. In most serious crashes, head injury is only one element of multiple serious injuries to various parts of the body, and is frequently not the sole cause of fatalities. The life-saving value of helmets is sometimes overstated, whilst the real-life experience of countries where the wearing of helmets has become more common suggests that, overall, head injury reduction is minimal.

British Standard BS6863 sets out minimum requirements for helmets, and if you decide to buy one you should ensure that it meets this or the more demanding Snell standard. However, the protection afforded by a helmet is very much dependent upon achieving a good fit. Heads are different, especially in the position of the chin relative to the skull, and a helmet which is suitable for one person may be quite unsatisfactory for someone else. Always buy a helmet from a shop where there is plenty of choice and where the sales staff are able to offer advice. Check for a snug and comfortable fit around your head, after making any internal adjustments. Alter the straps so that there is no slack in any of them (but the chin straps should not be uncomfortably tight), and then try to slide the helmet off. If it does not stay firmly in place, it is unsuitable for you.

Keeping the straps tight in use is extremely important. Not only can loose straps significantly reduce the protection given, by allowing the helmet to move on the head, but this in itself can also lead to serious neck injury. Research suggests that increased neck injury, due to badly fitted helmets, can cancel out any reduction in other types of head injury.

It is a particularly serious mistake to think that wearing a helmet is at all a substitute for learning to cycle properly. The protection offered by a helmet can easily be negated if you compensate by riding less carefully or if you find that wearing one interferes in any way with the attention that you are able to give to traffic. Ensure that a helmet will not interfere with your head movements, vision in any direction, hearing or the wearing of spectacles or sunglasses. Check also for general comfort, especially the adequacy of ventilation. Inadequate air circulation could impair your attentiveness on the road. Many cyclists who normally wear a helmet take it off when climbing hills in hot weather, and this is certainly preferable to overheating in a way that reduces concentration.

Helmets have only a limited effective life, even with careful use, and damage is not always visible. It is the condition of the crushable inner liner – usually made of polystyrene – that is most important, not the outer shell (if any). It is recommended that a helmet should be replaced at least every three years. If it is subjected to a hard drop or impact (inside or out) or becomes badly scratched, it must be replaced straight away. Chemicals, detergents, heat and sunlight can all reduce the strength of a helmet.

Mirrors

Many people coming to cycling after driving a car perceive the use of a rear view mirror as a safety aid. However, there are important differences between mirrors mounted on a car and those which can be attached to a cycle, and also between the amount and type of information that motorists and cyclists need to absorb from behind.

Cycles transmit vibrations from the road to a mirror much more actively than do cars. Also, cyclists change position relative to their vehicle more than car drivers. To look in a mirror, you must first change the focusing distance of your eyes from far to near, and then counter the vibration of the mirror image. This takes time, and as a result cycle mirrors are quite unsuited to giving you information quickly.

Mirrors, even if convex, have a limited field of view and

condense their image into a very small area. The driver of a wide vehicle, which acts as a physical barrier to others, is mostly concerned with what is happening to the rear; mirrors are therefore essential. However, a cyclist also needs to see clearly what is happening to the sides, and there are few occasions when looking behind in a mirror is sufficient. Turning your head is not only much quicker than looking in a mirror, it gives much more information about what is happening all around. It also gives more accurate information. For cyclists, the third dimension is all-important; judging the closing speed and distance of a following vehicle is much less easy in the small, two-dimensional image reflected by a mirror. Turning your head has other advantages over a mirror, such as alerting a following driver that you might be about to change course, and eye-to-eye contact with drivers is an essential part of negotiation.

Of course, looking behind can sometimes be tricky in dense traffic on narrow roads. An advantage of a mirror under these circumstances is to detect gaps in traffic that could allow you to look behind. There are other occasions, too, when a mirror might usefully supplement your awareness of traffic, and this is fine so long as your attention is not diverted from what's ahead and on riding a straight course. It is a mistake to think that you can look ahead and in a mirror at the same time.

Cycle mirrors are particularly unsuitable for use at night. Not only is it then even more difficult to discern detail in the reflected image, but the reflections of lights from vehicles behind can lead to dazzle, which is dangerous.

One situation in which a rear view mirror is to be recommended for a cyclist is when riding a recumbent cycle. Here, it can be more difficult to turn your body to look behind, and these machines sometimes allow the mounting of a mirror in a more satisfactory position.

Eye protection

Seeing where you are going is essential, not only for coping with traffic but to avoid riding off the road. Insects and smuts of airborne debris are potential dangers if trapped in an eye, although it is rare for both eyes to suffer simultaneously. Various eye shields, visors and glasses are sold to give protection, and could be useful if you find this a persistent problem, although you should make sure that the rims do not obstruct your peripheral vision.

Index